A MAN
A PLAN
A CANAL
PANAMA

For Tede Dorothy

with best wishes,

David

A MAN A PLAN A CANAL PANAMA

DAVID FLETCHER

Matador
9 Priory Business Park,
Wistow Road, Kibworth Beauchamp,
Leicestershire. LE8 0RX
Tel: 0116 279 2299
Email: books@troubador.co.uk
Web: www.troubador.co.uk/matador
Twitter: @matadorbooks

ISBN 978 1838590 529

British Library Cataloguing in Publication Data.
A catalogue record for this book is available from the British Library.

Printed and bound in the UK by TJ International, Padstow, Cornwall
Typeset in 11pt Aldine by Troubador Publishing Ltd, Leicester, UK

Matador is an imprint of Troubador Publishing Ltd

For Maggie and Lynette

2018

1.

With the help of KLM, Brian and Sandra had successfully managed to navigate their way from deepest Worcestershire to Tocumen International Airport on the outskirts of Panama City. Unfortunately, the driver of their transfer vehicle was having less success in navigating his way from the airport to their first scheduled lodge. In fact, when he finally undertook a U-turn on an anonymous tree-lined road, Brian decided that he was pretty well entirely lost.

Nevertheless, Brian was not unduly concerned. After all, Panama, as he knew, was not a very big country, and sooner or later their driver would no doubt track down their destination. Just as long, that is, as he remembered that Panama does not run from north to south, but instead from west to east. Not many people, Brian suspected, knew this, but it was simply a product of the geography of the New World. Put another way, if Panama ran south from its Central American neighbour, Costa Rica (rather than east), its lower bit would easily miss Colombia and its contiguous arrangement with South America would be completely scuppered. It would also mean, of course, that there would be a wide navigable channel between Panama and Colombia – and no need for the Panama Canal!

That would be pretty serious for Panama's economy, and it would also undermine the legitimacy of one of the longest palindromes in the world. That is to say that 'a man a plan a canal Panama' would essentially lose its meaning, and Brian would have to cast around for another equally impressive palindromic marvel. Which, of course, was all irrelevant stuff, but just the sort of musings that could infect Brian's mind when he was tired from a transatlantic flight and unsure of when he might be delivered to a much-needed bar-equipped refuge.

In any event, it soon transpired that the driver hadn't so much lost his way as momentarily mislaid it. Or maybe it was just that along that anonymous tree-lined road, there was only one turn-off that held out any prospect of his finding their lodge. So, having taken that unscheduled U-turn, he took this turn-off with only the slightest of hesitations. And it was, in fact, the beginning of a thin, winding road that went up and up and then up and up even further. Quite clearly, our two new visitors to Panama were being taken up a very large hill through the middle of a dense forest to what could only be their planned destination for today: the 'world-famous' Canopy Tower eco-lodge.

This lodge, Brian knew, was going to be interesting in its own right. And this was because it had started life not as an eco-destination but as a military installation. It had been built by the United States Air Force in 1965 to house a powerful radar used in the defence of the Panama

Canal. Thereafter it also took on a role in air traffic control and ultimately it played a part in detecting aeroplanes carrying drugs from South America. However, by 1995 it had become redundant, so that when in the following year its ownership passed from the USA to Panama, it was just an empty vacant building and it had to find itself a new role. This wasn't too difficult. Perched on the top of a hill with commanding views of the magnificent Soberania National Park within which it was located, it could only become one of the best situated eco-lodges in the world. It was not only in the right place, but its tower construction provided it with the sort of accommodation that would place its guests within the forest canopy itself. They would be only metres away from a multitude of both birds and animals. So, that's what happened. It was inaugurated as a lodge in 1999, since which time it has become a centre for neotropical-rainforest observation and eco-tourism like no other in the country. And, as Brian and Sandra were about to find out, its 'like no other in the country' credentials weren't necessarily exclusively good credentials…

They both got their first idea of the possibly negative aspects of a radar tower turned into an eco-lodge when the Tower first came into view. It was located within what looked like a copy of the original wire-fenced military compound (complete with military warning signs) – and it looked like a giant Coca-Cola can with an equally giant ping pong on its top (and to be entirely pedantic, that is like a giant Coca-Cola Life can – the lower-calorie version of Coke that comes in a green can). Yes, the Canopy Tower was a big, green metal can

– with windows in its sides, a big white sphere on its top, and with the very definite promise of a novel, not to say unique, experience within.

It didn't disappoint. The reception area, beyond a small, functional front door, had the air of an aircraft hangar, but one that had been pressganged into an alien use. Its entirely metal construction could not be concealed, and the installation of a rudimentary reception desk and a large 'naïve-style' mural depicting colourful examples of the local colourful wildlife only accentuated its workmanlike essence. Oh, and it was the shape of the inside of a can and there wasn't anybody behind the reception desk. All in all, it was an unusual, slightly disturbing and not very welcoming vestibule, and it certainly housed nothing from which a thirsty traveller might furnish himself – or herself – with some suitably stimulating refreshment.

This last feature of the reception area made it vital that Brian and Sandra should find someone to acknowledge their arrival, and with the help of their driver this someone was eventually found. He was a young chap who spoke very little English, but who was able to show his new visitors to their room – on the second floor – and to the lounge-cum-dining-area on the third floor. Both their room and the communal space at the top of the building succeeded in maintaining the lodge's novel-interior reputation.

Their room was a truncated segment of the tower, with a sliver to one side that contained a shower and those other pieces of porcelain that are necessary to maintain a clean and comfortable existence. In the principal segment

4

bit there were two beds, a couple of chairs, a desk and a hammock, and everywhere there was (very carefully-painted) metal. This formed the floor, the ceiling, the external walls – and those parts of the internal walls that weren't made up of old-fashioned wooden louvred panels. The overall ambience was of a steerage cabin on the Titanic, albeit one with windows and with too much space, and the overall concern of its new inhabitants was its acoustic characteristics. Would a bare metal room in a big metal can afford them any protection against the sounds of their shared accommodation?

By the time they had explored the lounge-cum-dining-area, this question had been answered. There seemed to be only three other guests in the lodge at the moment, but wherever one was in the building one would be aware of their individual whereabouts. The metal construction of the tower not only failed to insulate against sound, but it also served to amplify sound. Indeed, so much so that Brian suggested to Sandra that the Canopy Tower had probably not ever in its life hosted a successful union between a man and a woman – even if they'd tried it in one of the thoughtfully provided capacious hammocks.

However, it was gratification of another sort that was on Brian's mind at the moment, and having inspected the dining and lounging arrangements and having established that there was a bar – in the form of a help-yourself fridge packed with booze – he proceeded to achieve this gratification with a can of beer (and not with a can of Coca-Cola Life). Sandra joined him in this pursuit and then the two of them joined one of their fellow guests to explore the observation deck at the top of the tower.

This fellow guest was a German guy by the name of Christof – who turned out to be not only a very friendly German but also an outstanding wildlife artist – and the observation deck turned out to be outstanding full stop. It ran around the outside of the big ping pong ball and it provided a literally panoramic view of much of the tree-covered Soberania National Park as well as some enticing views of the abundant birdlife in the nearby trees. It was spellbinding and on its own well worth exposing oneself to the prospect of a less than serene (and likely celibate) environment for three days and nights.

The evening meal wasn't quite so spellbinding. Indeed, the food was dull and the company was worse than dull; it was essentially non-existent. While Brian and Sandra had earlier met a nice American couple, these two new acquaintances had sat at another table with Christof and three other guests who had arrived later. And this meant that they were obliged to share a table with a completely uncommunicative pair of ancient Germans. They were as rude as most of their fellow Germans were polite and friendly – like Christof – and Brian and Sandra would later learn that they had no interest whatsoever in wildlife! Quite why they were at the Canopy Tower was a real mystery. Just as was how they could be so thoughtless, inconsiderate and plain effing stupid when everybody had finally gone to bed…

The days started early in this eco-resort, which meant that all the inhabitants of the Tower retired to their rooms very early with the intention of getting off to sleep very early. This procedure underlined the absence of sound insulation in the tin-can tower, as all the retirees set about their night-time ablutions and inevitably made night-time ablutions sounds, all of which one could not fail to hear. Nevertheless, a sort of silence soon descended as all those in bed refrained from chatting or indulging in any other activity that might keep their companions awake. Unfortunately, however, this silence didn't last. It was the antediluvian oddities who had ignored Brian and Sandra at dinner. Only now they were ignoring the protocol being observed by all the other guests – and not by having noisy sex. No, what they were doing was having noisy conversations and sometimes noisy perambulations around their room, a room that was just next door to Brian and Sandra's.

Brian dealt with this initially by trying to ignore it. He then tried to manage his ire by whispering some well-chosen profanities to his wide-awake and equally perturbed wife. But in the end, sometime in the middle of the night, he was obliged to confront the problem head on – and in his underpants. He dressed (just enough to avoid arrest), left his room, took one pace to the door of the neighbouring room and banged on this door. He then informed the room's occupants that every word they said and every pace they took could be heard by all their fellow guests and that it would be a spiffing idea if they both just shut up and went to sleep. This exasperated announcement did not induce a response – and certainly not a revelation of his underpants to the German oldies – but it did cause them to pipe down. Indeed, when he'd returned triumphantly to his bed, they were so quiet that he did briefly entertain the thought that he'd been responsible for two cardiac arrests. And whilst this would be very unfortunate, it would at least mean that he wouldn't have to go through the same bothersome exercise in twenty-four hours' time.

Perhaps it was this gross insensitivity, or more likely the impact of carting one's old body over the Atlantic and several time zones, but Brian found that although in a now quiet room, he could not get to sleep. He needed, he decided, some sort of distraction, one that would enable him to ignore that his wife was already fast asleep and one that might let him drift into unconsciousness himself. And then he had it; he would devote a little of this middle of the night to reminding himself of why he had come to this Central American country in the first place. And so he did.

Well, the primary reason, he told himself, was that this modest-sized country, a nation only slightly bigger than Ireland, boasts a biodiversity that, on a per square-kilometre basis, may be more than twenty times that of Brazil. It is a bio-super-rich part of the world, and it owes this mega-diversity to its geological past. Put simply, North and South America were once joined, and then, because of some fidgeting in the Earth's crust, they weren't. About fifty million years ago they separated. And in their separated state they then proceeded to follow two very different evolutionary paths. South America took a route that delivered an astonishing variety of species, which today can be observed in creatures such as hummingbirds, iguanas, capybaras and poison-dart frogs. And during this same period, North America, which still rubbed shoulders with Eurasia, produced species that had no relatives in the southern continent – such as deer, raccoons, horses and mice. Then, like estranged lovers who finally realise that they have made a mistake, the South and the North got back together again. Some more fidgeting in the Earth's crust about three million years ago saw the formation of a new land bridge – in the shape of what would ultimately be named Panama – allowing the disparate species from both continents to mingle and for many of them to find a new home in the lush forests and wetlands of this brand new convenient isthmus. So Panama today has all the wildlife riches it could hope for. It has 220 mammal species, 162 amphibian species, 226 reptile species, nearly one thousand avian species, and 125 animal species that are found nowhere else on Earth. It also, of course, has that one dominant species that is screwing everything up around the world, and is not holding back locally. But, given this current musing was an exercise in distraction, Brian decided he would park the current destruction of the Panamanian environment and its constituent wildlife and revisit it another day – or another night. And anyway, he really had to learn to savour the good and ignore, as far as possible, the bad – starting early next morning when he and Sandra would make their first excursion into the Soberania National Park. Which, thanks to those two inconsiderate wrinklies, would now be in about three hours' time…

2.

At 6.30, Brian was still half asleep, but awake enough to wonder whether the vehicle parked outside the front door of the Tower was of the same vintage as the Tower itself. It did look rather military and it may well have seen service when this place was still operating as a radar installation. It certainly wasn't purpose built for the purpose to which it was now to be put – which was to convey five birders from the Canopy Tower, along a main road and into the heart of the Soberania National Park. It had an enclosed cab, which would be occupied by two of the Tower's resident guides, Georg and Igua, but behind it was just a raised deck surrounded by a metal handrail and, in the middle of the deck, a back-to-back double bench sitting at right angles to the cab. As Brian suspected and as was confirmed, as soon as this venerable vehicle was on that main road and travelling at speed, the bench configuration – and its exposure – provided a now silent bunch of birders with only a blur of passing vegetation, together with a cold-wind-tunnel experience on what, in the stationary world, was a hot and humid morning. There again, there was some relief to be had in observing other vehicles on the road, as they undertook overtaking

10

manoeuvres at a much greater speed and within what seemed like inches of those birders on the port side of the bench.

Brian was very happy when the vehicle drew to a halt at the beginning of the 'Pipeline Road'. This, as Brian and his fellow birders were already aware, was not a regular road but their destination for the day. And it was also another legacy of the US military.

Yes, during World War II, somebody had come up with the bright idea of building an oil pipeline across the Panama isthmus, just in case the canal was put out of action. And to lay a pipe, one, of course, first has to make a 'pipeline road'. This road still exists (as do remnants of the pipeline itself), and whilst it is now no more than a rough track through a forest, it is a track through the Soberania National Park – and through that part of it which constitutes one of the most bird-rich forests in the world. The track stretches for seventeen kilometres and it passes through a habitat which is characterised by its 'heterogeneity' – which is a posh way of saying that the habitat includes secondary growth, old growth, swamps and streams, and it is this habitat diversity that accounts for the exceptional bird life it sustains. (The bird species list for the 'road' now exceeds 400.)

Well, it was now time to put its remarkable credentials to the test, and thankfully this test would be conducted on foot. The intention was to stroll some way down the track very slowly before the birds disappeared in the midday heat, and then either stroll back or be ferried back in the birder-mobile if anyone was showing signs of heatstroke or exhaustion. The likelihood of that latter outcome was, in Brian's mind, very low. He was happy that he and Sandra wouldn't succumb to what would inevitably become sweltering temperatures, and the other three looked as though they could cope as well. These were Christof – who looked as though he could cope with anything indefinitely – and the American couple, who answered to the names of Steve and Jane, and who were clearly so enthusiastic about the forthcoming peregrination, that Brian doubted that they'd even notice the heat.

He was right on all counts. And those who had previously sung the wonders of the Pipeline Road were right on all counts as well. What this meant was that the group of five sauntered, ambled, pottered and dawdled all morning and without becoming distressed, and that with the help of their two guides they clocked up more birds than they could ever have hoped for along the length of the track. And what birds! All sorts of antwrens and antbirds, various woodcreepers, various puffbirds, a trio of different trogons and a whole string of others with equally ridiculous names. And whilst such treasures might fail to send the blood rushing around the veins of many, for the Pipeline five they brought a whole heap of delight, and easily enough delight to last them all day. Yes, it had to be admitted that it had been a physically demanding morning, especially if one's body had been assailed first by jetlag and then by enforced insomnia. Both Brian and Sandra had already decided that they would use the rest of the day to recuperate, and to recover from what was guaranteed to be another thrilling ride in the birder-mobile.

It *was* another thrilling ride in the birder-mobile. Georg and Igua had now loaded their pickup with the requisite number of guests and they were soon racing them back to the Tower in order that they could all dig in to a late lunch. It was as terrifying a trip as it had been on the way out, but Brian decided to provide himself with some relief, not by observing overtaking loonies, but by attempting to take in some of the sights that he'd ignored on the outward trip. This was well worth it, and particularly because part of the route home was next to the Panama Canal, and just before this route crosses the Chagres River (which feeds the entire canal system) one has the opportunity to observe one of the most remarkable cranes in the world. Not a sandhill crane or a blue crane or even a grey crowned crane – as, like other members of the *Gruidae* family, they are not found in Panama. No, the crane to be seen here is the Titan crane, one of the world's largest floating cranes that can lift up to 350 metric tonnes. It was one of three built in Hitler's Germany to lift up submarine sections and which, at the end of the war, were all carted off by the victors as war booty. The Russians took one, Britain took another (which it lost towing it across the English Channel in a storm!) and the US took the third. This last one worked in Long Beach, California for fifty years, and in 1999 it was shipped off to Panama, where it has since been used to lift the canal's lock gates when they are in need of refurbishment or repair. It was very definitely the biggest crane Brian had ever seen in his life – and maybe the oldest. And the fact that it was still working in the eighth decade of its life was quite remarkable and something of a testament to German engineering. Although, there again, thought Brian, it must be a real headache to find the right spares...

Tatiana agreed. She was the Canopy Tower's manager who had been absent yesterday but who had now returned to the lodge in all her sultry elegance to join the windswept visitors for their lunch. Her company was better than the food, and what was better than both was the opportunity to collapse on a bed and have a much-needed afternoon-long rest. Brian and Sandra both relished it greatly, and it was mostly undisturbed until it wasn't when some new arrivals turned up at the lodge at about 5.00. They were a contingent of American ladies with their guide and they came without a mute button.

Nevertheless, Brian and his wife were well revived by the time they reported for dinner, and this would be a dinner with Christof, Steve and Jane, and it would commence with an exchange of personal information and culminate with a discussion on the often-fraught relationship between Panama and the United States.

It was Brian's fault, really. After the main course he'd gone all didactic and had begun to tell the assembled company that almost immediately after Panama's independence from Spain in 1821, Panama had joined something called 'Gran Colombia', which was a confederation of Colombia, Bolivia, Ecuador, Peru and Venezuela, a united Latin American nation that had been the dream of Simón Bolívar. Of course, like most dreams it didn't last, and by 1831 all that remained was Colombia with Panama as a dependent province. This was significant, Brian explained while pouring himself more wine, because it was now dawning on the world that the narrow Panama isthmus was the obvious place to construct a crossing between the Atlantic and the Pacific, and this crossing was now needed more than ever.

At this point Steve interjected (and in doing so guaranteed that Brian's didacticism would now be sustained until after dessert), and his interjection was to underline this growing need for a crossing. As he explained, the 1830s and 1840s were a time when 'gold fever' was consuming the minds of many Americans, and by 1849, when the California gold rush got underway, tens of thousands of people travelled from the east coast of America to the west via Panama in order to avoid a lot of rather annoyed Native Americans in the middle of America. And they were able to do this because Colombia had signed a treaty with the US which permitted it to build a railway across the isthmus – and, significantly, to protect the railway with military force. The US and Panama had taken their first step on their long-lasting and very one-sided relationship.

Brian was gratified that this American at the table appeared to have the same view as himself of the intimate but intimidating nature of the US/Panamanian connection, and looked forward to Steve's further endorsement of his views. Because he now moved on to how the building of a railway inevitably led to talk about the building of a canal. Unfortunately, for Uncle Sam, he didn't get the job. Instead the Colombians gave it to this French guy who just happened to have built a canal through Egypt a few years earlier. So in 1881 the French started digging, but regrettably it didn't go terribly well, and by 1889 the French had screwed up completely. They were out of the scene, never to return.

Brian was now pouring wine again but he hadn't lost his thread. He was still able to inform his captivated table companions that this French cockup presented the Americans with what they saw as a lucrative opportunity, and they succeeded in persuading the French to sell them their concession for building the canal. Great – except that the Colombians wouldn't accede to this arrangement. So the scene was now set for a further step in the one-sided American relationship with Panama.

What they did was agree to the suggestion by the French company's chief engineer, a guy called Bunau-Varilla, to back a declaration of independence from Colombia by Panama, and in 1903 a revolutionary junta in Panama made this declaration. And then the US immediately recognised the new country's sovereignty. Then they did even more. They used some of their battleships to stop a seaborne contingent of Colombian soldiers from getting to Panama to put down the junta, and so guaranteed its rather token independence. Token, because Bunau-Varilla, now Panama's newly-appointed ambassador to the United States, hot-footed it to Washington before any mere Panamanians could organise a delegation, and signed a new treaty with the US which gave them the sort of rights that no genuinely sovereign nation would ever have agreed to. Not only would the Americans be building a canal, but they would also be receiving 'sovereign rights in perpetuity over the Canal Zone' (which extended eight kilometres on either side of the canal) *and* a broad right of intervention in Panamanian affairs!

Steve came back in at this point to admit that the US military did indeed repeatedly interfere in Panama's political affairs over the following years, and this eventually led to the watering down of US rights under the treaty – but not to its withdrawal from Panama. That would not come until 1999 when the canal passed to the Panamanian nation and all US military forces were withdrawn. And not before, as Steve reminded the table, the US had been obliged to respond to a declaration of war by that famous presidential drug dealer, one Manuel Antonio Noriega Moreno, with a devastating military attack on Panama City. But that, he suggested, was another story, and as it was now time for coffee, it was possibly time for another subject other than the asymmetrical bond between a small Central American country and a very large American one to the north.

Brian could only agree, and in any event he was beginning to feel tired again. He doubted he could sustain much more in the way of tuition this evening, and even if he could manage any at all, Sandra might suggest he didn't. She hadn't said anything, but she had that look on her face, that look which meant that it was well past the time that he pulled the plug. That he should limit his further contributions to the table to a thank you for the companionship provided during the meal and a wish that all those with whom he'd shared the meal would now have a restful and peaceful night. In short, say thanks, say goodnight and get up. Now.

This he did, and when back in their room, he made not a further mention of US/Panama antagonisms. Instead he just reminded Sandra that it was customary on their shared expeditions for him to provide her with some stimulating (intellectual) evening entertainment – and he had something in mind for their current expedition. Well, maybe the theme of the table discussion and the description of how one party can coerce another was still fresh in her mind. But for whatever reason, Sandra informed her husband that he could reveal his idea for entertainment tomorrow – but not tonight. And if he hogged the conversation again tomorrow evening then his announcement might be deferred indefinitely.

He got the message, said not another word – and instead began to relish the fact that in the next room that pair of elderly idiots had been replaced by a pair of clearly considerate American ladies. There was a real chance, he thought, of a peaceful and undisturbed night…

3.

*B*ill was an Englishman with whom Brian had yesterday had a very brief conversation. In this fleeting exchange he had learnt that this fellow guest at the Canopy Tower was due to leave early in the morning (that is to say this morning) in order to visit the Darién area of Panama (of which more later). What he had not learnt was that Bill was a self-setting human alarm clock. This only became apparent when Bill rose at 4.00 in the morning and took steps to ensure that his alarm function would operate effectively for the benefit of all those still asleep in their beds. He did this by embarking on a consultation with his wife at the top of his voice, which, given that she was still in England and on the other end of a mobile phone, might be considered by some to be mildly inconsiderate. Albeit he did have her on speaker, thereby allowing his recently-awoken victims to at least get both sides of this shouted conversation.

Never mind, by 4.15 he was on his way and peace returned to the Tower – for almost a couple of hours. Then it was time to get up and time for Brian and Sandra to savour the delights of the Soberania National Park for a second time. For a reason Brian could not bring to mind, today's excursion was to be with a private guide and, as was apparent when he and Sandra stepped outside the Tower, this meant that they were in for a treat. Because rather than yesterday's scary open-mobile, what was waiting to transfer them to the park was an enclosed-mobile, a regular, comfortable motor car. Air-conditioning would take the place of air-blasting, and accordingly Brian's mood lifted immediately. Indeed, it only dipped down again when he caught site of the observation tower…

Their driver, Ernesto, had brought Brian and Sandra to the park's 'Discovery Centre' – situated at the beginning of the Pipeline Road – and their guide, Roberto, had now brought them on foot to one of the Discovery Centre's principal attractions: its… towering 100-foot high observation tower. It seemed to go up forever – which is why, Roberto explained, it needed those 174 steps in its endless spiral staircase and why Brian felt rather more trepidation than excitement. Nevertheless, it was no time to act the wimp, and particularly as Roberto and Sandra were already on their way up the stairs. So Brian followed and after only a very short time, he was on the tower's observation platform and wondering whether his handkerchief could really do the job of two or three hand towels. It wasn't just that the climb up had made him sweat profusely, but now he was here, on a completely exposed platform under an already scorching sun, he knew he had a lot more sweat to come. It was absolutely roasting, even though it was still early in the morning. That said, it was also quite fabulous up on this platform. There were birds everywhere, and Roberto was able to find them all. There were more trogons, various parrots, beautiful caracaras, some of those remarkable toucans, a fabulous blue cotinga and so, so much more. It was a feast, but Brian being Brian, even a feast couldn't stop him thinking about not just the surrounding birdlife but also about what he was standing on. That is to say, he began to ponder how one goes about getting a 100-foot observation tower built. Where did the park authorities turn to when they decided they wanted such a structure in the middle of their domain? Brian had never seen any Yellow Pages entries for 'tower designers', and he doubted that even an internet search would throw up too many such outfits, especially in a place like Panama.

In the end, he decided that where one went to procure a designer/builder for one's observation tower would have to remain a mystery. It would have to be filed in that unsolved mystery file along with how women managed to knit, how programmes on baking cakes could possibly constitute a form of watchable entertainment and how fly-tipping has yet to be classed as a capital offence. Oh, and after this decision had been made, it was time to descend those 174 steps and to explore how a now very wet handkerchief could provide at least a modicum of blotting power. Even in the shade of trees back on the ground, it was still exceedingly hot.

Fortunately for Brian, there was plenty to provide a distraction from his award-winning leaking, and to start with it was some award-winning lekking, and all thanks to Roberto finding for his charges a splendid (male) golden-collared manakin. These tiny gold and black birds, like various other birds, indulge in an enthusiastic display – a lek – in order to attract a mate. And for this particular manakin, this involves its clearing a patch of ground beneath the undergrowth, and then its leaping around the patch while at the same time making a distinct clicking sound with its wings. It is the clicking sound which leads the female to the lek, and which enabled Roberto to find the lek so easily. It was then only a matter of getting down on one's knees to peer below the forest vegetation to catch a glimpse of this remarkable 'how about it, dear?' performance: an entrancing view of a tiny flash of gold, lighting up the undergrowth as it darted deftly about. Brian and Sandra were both deeply impressed, and Brian was deeply relieved that courting for his own species didn't involve a comparable amount of exertion on the part of the male.

There again, he would probably have opted for the degree of effort required of a golden-collared manakin in preference to the effort demanded of any of Panama's hummingbirds…

There were oodles of them around a feeding station below a thoughtfully provided viewing deck, and they were all whizzing around in that impossible way that always made Brian think that they were a product of some advanced bio-engineering. They were, he thought, more like some synthetic device that could have featured in *Blade Runner* than something that was purely natural. Maybe a flying eye for a future CIA agent, or even a miniaturised replacement for a secret agent, licenced to kill, or at least to sup sugar-water from suspended feeders. And one of them in particular was quite clearly entirely unnatural. This was a diminutive chap called a rufous-crested coquette. And that is diminutive in the sense that this particular hummingbird is about the same size as a large boiled sweet, but unlike a large boiled sweet, it comes complete with an extravagant Mohican-style rufous crest and it has all the whizzing and impossible-manoeuvring capabilities of its fellow hummingbirds. It would have no problem in ranking as Brian's 'best bird of the day' – with the golden-collared manakin coming in a close second.

The 'best *meal* of the day' was lunch. This consisted of mustard-topped cheese and ham sandwiches, made on the spot by Roberto and consumed at a wooden table near the Discovery Centre's shop. They were delicious, as were some of the sights that presented themselves during the meal. Because this national park, despite its size and its formidable credentials, is really very close to Panama City, and it therefore attracts what can only be called day-trippers. This means that as well as khaki-covered, binocular-draped birders, the Discovery Centre hosts some distinctly 'non-birders' in their shorts, tee-shirts, flip-flops – and very well-tanned skins. Brian was heartened to see them. The joys of places such as this should be relished by all, not just by middle-aged amateur ornithologists – even if some of the non-birders looked even more ridiculous than the birders...

Well, lunch was followed by a short walk up the Pipeline Road, but it was now blisteringly hot, and the birds had all retired for a siesta, which is what Brian and Sandra did when they were deposited back at the Canopy Tower. And almost inevitably, this siesta took them to aperitifs time, in the shape of a lager each, and after this there was another meal with Steve and Jane.

This proved to be the 'worst meal of the day' in food terms, but in terms of banter and overall enjoyment, it fared a great deal better. Brian didn't slip into didactic mode, which was as welcome as it was rare, but he did participate in a lively discussion about humour. This was kicked off by Steve, who was interested to know which, if any, American humour found favour with his two English table companions. It was soon established that as well as *M★A★S★H*, *Parks and Recreation* went down well in the Brian and Sandra household, and that its principal performer, Amy Poehler, could not fail to be recognised as a naturally funny character in any English-speaking society. *Fawlty Towers* and the much more recent *Upstart Crow* found similar acceptance in the Steve and Jane household, and this led on to which individual comics worked well on either side of the Atlantic.

Ricky Gervais featured in this discussion, as did John Cleese (almost inevitably), but so too did John Lithgow and Rik Mayall. All of these chaps got pretty well top marks, but there were others who got a mention but who failed to win transatlantic approval, largely because they hadn't made it across the pond. Significant amongst these were people like Lee Mack and Jack Dee. And, as much as he tried, Brian was unable to convince anybody, including Sandra, of the comedic genius of Dianne Abbott. Despite his pushing the point that Dianne could put on a 'political' performance that was funnier than anything the BBC was currently providing in its so-called comedy output, he just couldn't win his argument. Even when he told his table audience that Dianne was planning to team up with the retired John Prescott to form a new 'Abbott and Prescotostello' comedy duo, they just wouldn't have it.

Nevertheless, the conversation at the table had been a good one and, as it didn't include a potted history of US/Panama relationships, it even allowed Brian to get Sandra back to their room in time to once again broach the subject of her intellectual evening entertainment. And he wouldn't allow her to get away with a deferral again!

He launched into his assault as soon as they were tucked up in bed.

'OK,' he started imaginatively. 'In the past, I've done a demolition job on a collection of various countries. I've done the merits of the Seven Deadly Sins. And I've done "interesting facts" about the nations of South America…'

'Which really is more than enough,' interrupted Sandra.

At this point Brian indulged in a fleeting scowl but carried on as if Sandra had made no interruption at all.

'So…' he continued, 'I thought it was about time to remind you, each evening, of something that has now disappeared from our lives. You know, things that have gone, the passing of which we may have hardly noticed, but the former existence of which we should never forget…'

'Oh my God…'

'And I thought…'

'Hold on, Brian,' interrupted Sandra again, 'you're not seriously planning to resurrect the past, when there is so much of the present to enjoy. And more to the point, when there is so much imminent sleep to enjoy?'

'Yes,' responded Brian cheerily, 'and I thought I would start with a short one – on antimacassars…'

It was no use. Sandra just sighed and let her husband carry on.

'Right. Well, as I'm sure you'll remember, our childhoods were spent in homes where little decorative pieces of cloth adorned the back of every armchair and every settee. Antimacassars were as vital to wholesome fifties and sixties domesticity as were Harpic and Dettol.'

'Brian…'

'And I'm sure you might also remember that the Macassar to which these cloths were the *anti*-dote, so to speak, was Macassar oil, a commonly used *unguent* for the hair commonly used throughout the Victorian period…'

'I did…'

'But you might not remember that the antimacassar word also refers to the wide cloth collar on a sailor's shirt designed to keep the oil off his uniform. Or that Byron made a reference to "thine incomparable oil"…'

'Brian!'

'What?'

'I want to go to sleep. And anyway, they haven't disappeared. Go on any plane or any train…'

'That's not the same. It can't be. I mean…'

'Sleep, Brian. I said sleep.'

'Right,' Brian responded. 'I…'

'Won't say another word. Yes. I know. Now, please go to sleep. You know we have to be asleep before somebody can wake us up. If we're awake already, it isn't anything like as much fun, is it?'

Brian managed an almost whispered, 'No, dear,' bade his wife a fond goodnight, and then set about thinking what subject he should choose for tomorrow's brief dissertation. And on the basis of Sandra's reaction this evening, it probably shouldn't be Bakelite ashtrays or even illuminated cocktail cabinets. He would give it some thought. Just as soon as he'd given a great deal more thought to that incredible rufous-crested coquette…

*B*rian woke up feeling a little disturbed that he hadn't been disturbed in the night. However, this confusion soon passed and soon after this, he and Sandra were up on the Tower's observation deck with Jane, Steve and Georg, making the most of what would be their final couple of hours in this unique destination. It was well worth it. In the early-morning light, the surrounding forest views were sublime, and the forest itself was full of life – and of one particularly loud form of life: howler monkeys. Out there, there were at least two groups of these local mantled howler monkeys. They were not especially close to the Tower, but both groups were demonstrating only too clearly how these animals have earned their name. Their calls are quite remarkable; creatures with a body length of about two feet, capable of emitting a huge sonorous bark that one would expect to hear from something the size of King Kong. Their rich, resonant 'wall of sound' is quite extraordinary and, for those who hear it for the first time, more than a little scary. One could well imagine that one was being approached by a band of monstrous animals, recently escaped from the pages of some overblown sci-fi thriller, and not by some completely harmless mammals, whose only terrifying trait is the sporting of a white scrotum by the adult males. And that's hardly terrifying at all. Hell, who hasn't at some time been confronted by a white scrotum?

Anyway, as well as the howlers there was lots of birdlife around, and it was a constant struggle to keep up with Georg as he pointed out yet another spectacular manifestation of Panama's avian inhabitants. There were red-rumped caciques, brown-headed parrots, black-headed tody-flycatchers, and green honeycreepers, to name but a few, but unfortunately – for Brian – nothing referred to as beige. And he'd so wanted to clock a bird that had beige in its name, or even better, one with shocking-pink in its title. Perhaps, he thought, he might just have to wait for a new species to evolve…

Happily, no such wait was required for the scheduled transfer to the next lodge, another place in the Canopy family, called (unchallengingly) 'Canopy Lodge'. This hostelry is situated just outside El Valle de Antón, a town sitting in a flat, wide caldera (of the reassuringly dormant El Valle volcano) about two hours by road to the west of the Tower. And accordingly, at about 9.00am, a car pulled up outside the Tower's front door to whisk Brian and Sandra to this next birdy destination. After a round of goodbyes (and a photo with Tatiana to go on Facebook!) Brian and Mrs Brian inserted themselves into this car, and the car pulled away. They were now on their way, and on their way to see an entirely new aspect of Panama, one that would be seared into their minds for some time to come.

Now, before describing this aspect, it is probably time to admit that Brian had a string of unique qualifications.

That is to say that having achieved an 'A' in A-level litter studies, he went on to university to do a degree in rubbish, and from there to complete a doctorate in 'trashing the environment' at the world-renowned Grot University. Since then he has made various expeditions around the world to investigate and document the tidal wave of garbage that is being allowed to overwhelm it and to reduce it to a dross-covered landscape of which every human being should be ashamed. Oh, and he had earlier picked up a badge in woodcraft and emergency splints.

So, ignoring the woodcraft and emergency splints qualifications, it is only too apparent that Brian can claim to have more than a passing interest in litter and its associated consequences as well as an extensive experience of all its terrible manifestations all over the planet. Nevertheless, what he was to experience on the two-hour trip to El Valle de Antón was like nothing he'd seen before. And this was because a large part of this journey was along the famous Pan-American Highway – or at least a stretch of that part of it which runs through the nation of Panama – and what edged this cool-sounding thoroughfare was an effing disgrace.

Shortly after crossing the Panama Canal, Brian and Sandra found themselves exposed to this linear disfigurement of the planet. And it was continuous. It ran for miles as the constant border to the highway: piles of rubble, drifts of assorted litter, mounds of discarded building material, endless heaps of breezeblocks, jumbles of tyres, corrugated iron, oil drums, beer crates, dumped vegetation and indeed just about every sort of junk one could imagine, including literally hundreds of abandoned vehicles and thousands of vehicle bits. There was, it has to be admitted, a modicum of relief from this unceasing desecration of the environment if, that is, one could regard any number of astonishingly ugly, garishly-coloured, semi-derelict houses as some sort of relief. Or even the rows of dismal, filth-surrounded workshops, or maybe the scores of equally dismal and disorganised builder's yards. So not much in the way of relief at all really...

Of course, there will be apologists who seek to explain this sort of rampant 'untidiness' and its associated ugliness by pointing to the impact of poverty, and to an extent this is a valid argument. Poor people have more pressing issues to deal with than managing their waste. However, as observed by Brian on many of his previous expeditions, it now seems to have become acceptable, in so much of the world, for all sorts of waste not to be managed at all but simply to be discarded and then ignored. And, furthermore, for the resulting ugliness to be mirrored in the abandonment of any attempt to recognise the importance of aesthetics in the design of domestic or commercial property. So much of what is built is unsightly to start with and then even more unsightly as it is used and abused. And, unfortunately, the people of Panama seem to have embraced this new way of thinking with respect to waste and building design with wide-open arms. If one set out with the primary purpose of designing the most hideous-looking margins for this nation's primary thoroughfare, then one would be hard put to better what had already been achieved through years of wanton neglect and a wanton blindness to ugliness in all its forms. Poverty wasn't the problem here (at least, not all of it), but it was 'attitude', a communal dereliction of duty in respect of the need to care for one's immediate environment (let alone the wider environment).

It was all very depressing – for poor old sensitive Brian – and it wasn't until the Pan-American Highway was abandoned in favour of a much narrower road that he began to revive. This was the route to El Valle de Antón, and whilst it wasn't the most picturesque (or litter-free) route imaginable, it was a big improvement on what had been experienced so far. And when it led into El Valle de Antón itself, it was as though that unfortunate attitude responsible for Brian's earlier distress had disappeared entirely. The town was almost pretty and it certainly reflected a cared-for approach by its 8,000 inhabitants. It was no surprise then, that Canopy Lodge, just out of town, was what might be described as a model of order and charm.

It was situated just beyond the clearly well-off fringes of the town, and it was approached along a winding path through its gardens that eventually took Brian and Sandra across a beautiful stream and into its open-fronted dining area. Whilst El Valle de Antón is 600 metres above sea level and therefore appreciably cooler than the Soberania National Park, its climate still allowed *al fresco* catering, albeit *al fresco* with appropriate shelter to recognise the frequency of rainfall in the area.

Anyway, first impressions were very favourable, and they remained favourable when Brian and Sandra were taken to their room, a generous chamber complete with a covered balcony – and with no evidence of metal in its construction. Canopy Lodge not only looked rather more conventional than Canopy Tower, but it also promised a rather better acoustic experience than that provided by its Coke-can cousin to the east. It didn't seem, however, that it promised a great deal of improvement in terms of food, at least not judging by what was on offer at lunchtime.

It was a distinctly bland offering, relieved only by (part of) the company at Brian and Sandra's table. There were four fellow diners, all American (as were all the other guests at the lodge) and two were sisters-in-law and really good fun, and the other two were completely unrelated brothers-in-law and were not good fun. They were just humourless and their most interesting feature was that they were both about six-foot-six. They were like tall negatives of John Cleese, and Brian just knew that even their funny walks wouldn't be very funny.

It was fortunate then that the two sisters-in-law, Mary and Kathy, were in attendance. Indeed, they were such good fun that the afternoon turned into a brief interlude between lunch and dinner, when these two delightful ladies suggested that they again shared Brian and Sandra's table, but this time without the lanky duo. It wasn't, of course, an entirely empty interlude, in that Brian and Sandra inspected the lodge's grounds and thereby spied a wonderful grey-headed wood rail, an equally wonderful rufous-capped warbler and a superb rosy thrush-tanager – and they also had a short siesta. But it did seem like an interlude, so enjoyable was the experience of the evening meal, and again despite the food and due solely to the presence of a pair of ideal dinner companions.

Much of what was discussed with these two attractive ladies would soon become lost in a red-wine-induced haze, but it definitely included some reminiscences by the 'mature-hippy', Mary and her equally mature and bubbly sister-in-law, Kathy. It also, almost inevitably, involved a denial of any responsibility on their part for That Really Unutterably Malevolent President, and an exposition on their disbelief that so many of their fellow Americans could have voted for the nastiest narcissist on the block – and not yet realised the consequences of their dreadful mistake. Of course, Kathy and Mary were not the first Americans to have expressed these views. So too had Steve and Jane back at Canopy Tower – and, to their credit, the two Cleese-lookalikes, and every other American Brian and Sandra had met on their current expedition, and every other American they had recently met in Africa. And who could blame any of them? And who could forgive any of those other stay-at-home Americans who had inflicted this ridiculously coiffured disaster on their country? Hadn't they looked at him? Hadn't they listened to him? Hadn't they thought for one second that electing an ignorant charlatan to the presidency might not be such a good idea?

Anyway, dinner was great and it succeeded in erasing any thoughts of disfigured highways – but not Brian's promise to himself that he would enlighten his wife on another aspect of past life that has now been lost for all time. And this was the commonplace employment of suspender belts by the majority of women to hold up their stockings.

Now, he had to be careful here. He knew he was dealing with a potentially sensitive subject and one that could blow up in his face. He therefore adopted an approach that didn't so much regret the passing of the suspender era for the loss of titillation it provided, but more for the loss of the demarcation zone it provided. He explained this to Sandra as follows:

'You see, that upper thigh area, those two bands of bare flesh both crossed by those stretched but delicate underpinnings, were a delineation of sorts. Below this "suspenseful strip" one knew one was on reasonably safe ground. But one also knew that beyond that strip there was something as dangerous as it was mysterious, and that if one ignored the delineation afforded by that outpost of supporting underwear one could get into real trouble…'

At this point Sandra began shaking her head.

'But then, when mini-skirts and tights came along, it all went wrong. The demarcation zone disappeared, and there was no longer an advance warning that there was something to take notice of ahead. Legs simply merged into upper legs – and so on – and both men and women soon began to see no distinction between… well, what and where was decent and what and where was potentially very indecent. Suspenders had gone and so too had a recognised border, one defined by naked flesh and taut ribbons. And that was it: nothing less than the beginning of the end for traditional decency and established morality.'

Sandra shook her head some more. Then she spoke.

'You've never worn the damn things,' she said. 'If you had, you would understand why they are now not commonplace anymore. And you certainly wouldn't want to see them reintroduced just so some lecher could gauge how bloody lecherous he was being.'

'Well, I…'

'And for God's sake, you seem to be suggesting that any degree of fumbling up to a woman's stocking tops was quite OK, and only when no-man's land came into view were you supposed to consider your actions. And as for all that nonsense about the downfall of morality, well that's all it is: nonsense. You'll be suggesting next that the demise of conical bras led to the onset of feminism and the beginnings of the gender identity crisis…'

'Well, I…'

'…don't know what I am talking about. Yes, I noticed…'

'Well, I…'

'You're not suffering from altitude sickness, are you?'

'We're only at 600 metres.'

'Yes, and we're only at day four of a three-week expedition. I dread to think what you've got in store for me yet.'

Brian decided against telling his wife what he had in store for her yet. He didn't think it was quite the best time to do that. Instead, he bade Sandra a peaceful good night and gave a last few thoughts to suspenders and stockings. Maybe, he admitted to himself, his analysis of the impact of their demise could be challenged, but he still thought they had an undeniable attraction. In the same way that LPs still had an undeniable attraction. Or, there again, maybe not in quite the same way that LPs still had an undeniable attraction. Maybe there was a subtle distinction…

And then he was asleep.

5.

He didn't stay asleep all night. He was awoken by the noise of a violent wind in the middle of the night and again, towards morning, when the wind was joined by a brief but very noisy bout of torrential rain. There was clearly a conspiracy going on to ensure that his Panama nights were disturbed as often as was credibly possible.

Anyway, he and Sandra still managed to make breakfast by 6.30, feeling reasonably rested. And after breakfast it was time to embark on their first excursion of the day: a guided walk with Ken and Jack, the unfunny brothers-in-law from yesterday's lunch. Their initial destination was some sort of collection of waterfalls, and this was to be reached by strolling up the road outside the lodge and away from what were the furthest fringes of El Valle de Antón. It was a stroll that revealed a number of things. The first was that the road outside the lodge rose quite steeply. The second was that there were quite a few birds about. And the third was that Ken and Jack were keen bird photographers – but not that enthusiastic to recognise that they constituted only half of the party. Accordingly, they had soon recruited Tino, the guide, to their exclusive cause, and it began to feel to Brian as though he and Sandra were just afterthoughts. And this he didn't much like at all.

There again, he reminded himself, being side-lined on a birding walk wasn't exactly the worst thing in the world. It wasn't as though he and Sandra had been duped into a temperance holiday in Rhyl or an evangelical jamboree in Hull. And it was a million miles away from something like having been born into a religion from which one couldn't escape. So, he came to terms with it and, with Sandra, reconciled himself to their current situation and just focused on enjoying their jaunt – if necessary, entirely on their own.

It worked. When they reached the 'waterfalls' (which were a series of pools in the same stream that passed the lodge, a little further up its course), he and his wife found that they could enjoy all on their own a nesting sun bittern that was found there. And they could even ignore Ken and Jack's attempt to monopolise the best viewing spot. Furthermore, Brian was able to take on the mantle of guide himself, by informing Sandra that the closest relative of this South and Central American bird is the almost flightless kagu, a bird he and his wife had failed to see in New Caledonia the previous year. And did she know, he wondered, that these two birds formed an exclusive Gondwanan lineage along with a family of birds called *Mesites* found only in Madagascar? She did not, but she did know that a Gondwanan lineage meant that their ancestors were from Gondwanaland, which of course meant that they had a very long lineage indeed – and that this nesting lady's ancestors must have been around tens of millions of years before Panama even existed. It was an intriguing thought, but not one shared with Ken and Jack. They were too busy with their expensive cameras, cameras that would probably prove their worth when they were deployed in securing pictures of this morning's primary 'target bird'. And it was now time, Tino decided, to search for this bird.

Now, it should be recognised at this stage that the stretch of the 'waterfalls' stream that was currently being investigated for its wildlife ran through an area of dense, shadowy vegetation. Furthermore, this vegetation covered the sides of the valley through which the stream ran and therefore edged the narrow, steep path up which Tino now took his four somewhat apprehensive charges. And they were right to be apprehensive. The path was not only steep and narrow, but it was also extremely slippery and it offered to its users a readily available multiple-injury outcome, should they lose their footing and descend rapidly fifty or more metres through that dense but not necessarily cushioning vegetation. It was pretty scary and got scarier the further up the trail Tino took them. However… it was all in a good cause, and the cause was to find a tiny little bird who just happens to like dense, shadowy vegetation. And this was the morning's target bird – the super-diminutive, super-furtive tody motmot.

It is real. Despite its name, it is not a made-up cartoon bird on some children's TV channel, and it is of course a real charmer – when it can be seen. This is not often as it really is a very furtive bird indeed, and it needs a practised guide who can mimic its call to stand any chance of it being brought out of the dense vegetation and into view. Tino was one such guide, and just as Brian had come to the conclusion that the next stretch of the path looked plainly lethal, Tino must have made out a motmot's distinctive whistling song. Because he immediately commenced to imitate it perfectly, and by doing so brought the required tody motmot out and onto a nearby branch and into full view of the now clearly impressed party. It was so close that binoculars were not required, but with its not particularly colourful plumage and with little light under the forest canopy, those expensive cameras certainly were. Ken and Jack were soon clicking away like mad.

It was a good outcome for all concerned, especially when another tody motmot came along to get his own photo taken, and even more so when all five in the party managed to get down the path without breaking any limbs. Now it was easy going again, first back up along the stream and then along another path, this one not nearly so steep and in no way so daunting, but instead rewarding. And this was because Tino was able to find for the birding quartet a mottled owl, a medium-sized owl that apparently spends much of its life perched on its chosen branch. Consequently, if, as a guide, one knows where this branch is, and it is the right time of day, one can pretty well guarantee that one will be able to show it to one's charges. The trick, Brian concluded, was finding the particular branch in the first place. And the next trick, for Tino, was to occupy his small team of birders with just enough diversions to take them to lunchtime. This involved him taking them away from the 'waterfalls', further up the road and then back down again, but with no great reward. The birds had gone into 'hide mode' and there was nothing to see – or to be snapped. Even Ken and Jack were becoming bored.

So, by 1.00 they, together with Brian and Sandra, were sitting down for a shared lunch (the rest of the guests having been taken off for a whole-day expedition to the coast to the south). This didn't prove as awful as Brian had feared, due principally to his seeking out topics for their over-lunch conversation that would not be controversial, topics such as the nonsense of regarding the wanton killing of animals as a sport.

He kicked off this conversation by suggesting that he could simply not understand how a rational human being could find some sort of pleasure in ending the life of a fellow creature, when that creature wasn't vital to the sustenance of life and hadn't caused anyone any harm. Ken responded to this observation by declaring that 'sport hunters' probably had a mental disorder. Brian agreed but attempted to more closely define this disorder by making reference to the hunters' genitals. They 'sported', he opined, a penis that was either too small or too misshapen for comfortable use. Or... he conceded, they might sport a penis that simply didn't work, and was only good for wetting themselves when they were scared – which was on occasions such as their meeting an attractive young woman or simply when they were on their own without any of their sport-hunter friends.

At this point Jack made the observation that some sport hunters were women, to which Brian responded that it was still down to a problem with genitals. More specifically, he suggested that if, as a woman, your own trigger doesn't work, you seek out one that does – even if it means the demise of some poor, innocent animal who has no such problems with its own genitalia. And as often as not the poor, innocent animal will be a lot more physically attractive than its murdering huntress.

Brian could sometimes be mildly controversial in his views, but not on this occasion. Nobody at the table challenged what he'd said – and Sandra agreed with him wholeheartedly. She also agreed to his idea of a post-lunch semi-lazy afternoon, and as soon as lunch was concluded this got underway. It did involve some walking, and this was first to the lodge's splendid treehouse and then to its kitchen's fruit and vegetable dump, a large pile of organic detritus hidden away in the lodge gardens. Here were found a whole clutch of new birds, including the sadly named – but really rather handsome – clay-coloured thrush. Following this was some sitting – and some observing of the lodge's bird-feeders, where there was a never-ending procession of new birds, and probably more than had been observed on this morning's walk…

From what was reported by the returned Americans before dinner, even a full-day's birding wouldn't necessarily yield more bird species than a well-established feeding station in the right location, but it would generate a good appetite. There was a palpable urgency to sit down for the evening meal – and a matching desire on the part of Kathy and Mary that their meal should again be shared with just Brian and his equally thirsty spouse.

43

So excessive-wine-consumption-meal number two got underway, and it kicked off with an observation by Kathy that Brian appeared to be keen on wearing tee-shirts, because, just like last night, he was kitted out in one of these garments. Brian responded to this observation by admitting that he was doing no more than exercising his rights as a citizen of Britain – under its unwritten constitution – to 'bare arms'. And this in some way led to his suggesting that hunters in America might come to their senses if the American constitution included the right to 'arm bears'. Getting those defenceless targets to start shooting back might make all the difference in the world.

This was when Sandra suggested that this idea could be rolled out across the world, and that in a place like Panama, much of the present degradation of its natural wonders could be brought to a stop if the representatives of its wildlife were equipped with some appropriate weapons. How about some small pistols for the local opossums, some AK47s for the prowling howlers, and maybe some old-fashioned hand grenades for the various parrots – the pins of which they could easily extract with their beaks before dropping said ordnance on the heads of both insufferable hunters and illegal loggers?

These proposals were not entirely sensible and they were clearly a little too close to the idea of arming teachers in American schools. Nevertheless, they had to be toasted by the assembled four – more than once. Which is probably why Brian could not recall absolutely every detail of the following three hours of conversation and why it took him a little time back in his bed to bring to mind what he needed to impart to Sandra in respect of his next 'stuff that was with us but is with us no more'. Silly really, because it was such an obvious example of what has been lost. It was 'pipes', and that is 'pipes', not as in the Pipeline Road, but 'pipes' as in what boffins used to puff on as they invented things like bouncing bombs, and Labour Prime Ministers used to puff on as they invented new ways to wreak havoc on our nation and its faltering economy.

Anyway, he eventually got himself together and he started with an admission.

'You know,' he said, 'I don't think I've ever sucked on a pipe.'

'You've never sucked on what?' responded Sandra.

'A pipe. You know, a tobacco pipe, one of those polished briar-wood things that used to adorn many a suburban sitting room – and stink them out something rotten.'

'Why are you telling me this?'

Brian adopted an affronted expression. Had his wife already forgotten the theme of his evening entertainments?

'It's my next example of what has gone from our lives. I mean, fags have receded into the shadows, but pipes have become virtually extinct. I mean, when was the last time you saw anybody smoking a pipe?'

'Last Thursday. There was a guy on a bench in the middle of Droitwich.'

Brian looked affronted again. Then he regrouped.

'Ah, but I bet he was old, wasn't he? Some old codger who hasn't realised that pipes are now entirely passé.'

'He was younger than you.'

Brian bristled.

'Look,' he said, 'I think we're getting off the point.'

'Which is?'

'Which is… that pipes used to be an integral part of the lives of millions of men, and part of the backdrop to our own lives, but now…'

'…they're only in the middle of Droitwich.'

'No. I mean, well, yes. They're now very rare. You hardly ever see them…'

'And never if you keep your eyes closed, like I'm doing now, in the vain hope of being allowed to get to sleep. I mean, for God's sake, Brian, we polished off four bottles of wine this evening and just at the moment I have a far greater interest in your piping down than in your talking to me about pipes. And what that means in simple English is please shut up and go to sleep.'

Brian had no option but to accede to this request – and he was, after all, pretty knackered himself. Walking, climbing up impossible paths and alcoholic beverages could, taken together, have quite a knackering effect. He was, however, a little annoyed that his dissertation on pipes had been cut so short and that he hadn't been able to ask his wife whether she thought that there might be a pipe-smoking habit, no matter how small, in this Central American country. And if there was, whether their implements might possibly be referred to as 'Pan pipes'.

Maybe he'd ask her in the morning – or maybe he wouldn't. Probably the latter…

6.

*B*rian awoke feeling less than entirely rested. There had been a storm overnight and this had kept him awake. He had eventually fallen asleep, but he had then awoken in a sweat as a result of a dream. It was more a nightmare really, because its theme was the installation of Jeremy Corbyn as the Commander-in-Chief of the British Armed Forces. He knew, even in the dream, that this position was vested in the monarch, but he also knew that the real authority for these forces was vested in the Prime Minister of the day – and that meant that there was rather too much reality in this dream for his liking. The idea of a closet Trotskyist being in control of the country's army, air-force and navy was sphincterally alarming. It was like making Tracey Emin the director of the National Portrait Gallery, only about a thousand times worse – and it was absolutely guaranteed to rouse him from his slumbers.

So… the day didn't get off to a good start, particularly as it was still raining in the morning and still drizzling when a new guide called Daniel installed (just) Brian and Sandra into his awaiting transport. He was to take them much further up the road outside the lodge so that they could conduct a new round of birding in the highlands above El Valle de Antón, where there would be a new mix of birds. However, this was when things took a turn for the better, and they took a turn for the better because as well as Daniel being very welcoming and very cheerful, the interior of his small Toyota sedan had been pimped in pink. It had a big pink dangly thing hanging from the rear-view mirror, a fluffy pink steering-wheel cover and, most incredible of all, the end of its gear lever had been sheathed in what looked like a pink, heavily-ribbed condom. On this grey, drizzly morning, the assemblage of pink – and particularly that shocking-pink prophylactic – could not fail to have brightened Brian's mood and to have driven from his mind any residual thoughts of trouble with Trots. Oh, and then the birding proved pretty remarkable as well.

It started a mile or so up the road, just outside a half-derelict house, occupied by what Brian assumed must be a family of deaf people. Their radio was on so loud that it must have been audible in Costa Rica, but it didn't seem to bother the birds. They were everywhere: tanagers, saltators, vireos, euphonias, warblers and a host of others. They darted about within the drizzle and brightened up the morning even more than all that pink. And there was still more to come.

There were a couple of new birds further up the road – next to the local chicken factory (!). Daniel had stopped near to this enormous incongruous enterprise (surrounded by lawns and flower beds) and had taken Brian and Sandra for a short walk here. When they'd completed that, he then drove them to a stretch of road that ran through a dense forested area of the uplands, and there were further birds here. Indeed, a lot more birds here. It seemed as though it was a super-hotspot for warblers and hummingbirds. And, of course, Daniel was super-proficient in being able to find them all and then point them out.

It was the same when he then took his charges onto a trail in another part of the uplands. This was cut through a mist-covered forest and its gently rising gradient required only a modicum of effort in exchange for some generous rewards. To start with there was a beautiful tawny-crested tanager and an orange-bellied trogon, and then there was a black guan! Heck, this was something to get quite excited about, even if one didn't suffer from OBD (obsessive birding disorder) because this was a black, turkey-sized bird that is rarely seen as it hauls its turkey-sized body through the canopy of the montane forests of just Panama and Costa Rica in search of the fruits and berries on which it feeds. It is the most discreet arboreal (rather than terrestrial) frugivorous heavyweight one could possibly encounter in this upland area of the country, and there is little doubt that in the near future it will become ever more difficult to find. It prefers intact, undisturbed forests and, needless to say, it will very soon run out of these. Not surprisingly it is therefore threatened by habitat loss and is officially classed as 'near-threatened' because of its limited range. So, all in all, a wonderful spot and at the same time a reminder of the fragility of what makes the world special.

Something else that makes the world special is a little chap called a white-tipped sicklebill, a diminutive hummingbird that is easily recognisable by its… sickle-shaped bill, a sharp and extremely curved bill that bends almost into a right angle. And it has evolved into this shape to allow the sicklebill to feed on the nectar of certain tubular-shaped flowers, flowers of plants such as those in the genus *Heliconia*. Fortunately for Brian and Sandra, there was an example of this genus in this upland forest, a variety by the name of *Heliconia rostrata* (otherwise known as hanging lobster claw) – and Daniel knew where to find one such particular plant. There he stationed his two English visitors and after only a few minutes a white-tipped sicklebill arrived and began to feed. It was a stunning sight and it constituted a splendid full stop to their morning's birding – just before the drizzle decided it was time to become full-blown heavy rain.

It became so heavy that the two birders and their guide had to hurry back to the road and there seek shelter in a disused… bus shelter (which, by the way, was far too small ever to have given shelter to a bus). And there Brian and Sandra waited for the rain to ease before walking back to Daniel's car, passing the time by chatting to Daniel and by sharing his stock of (mixed) nuts, raisins and M&Ms, a combination of the savoury and the sweet that they had never before encountered.

What they had encountered before was a duo by the name of Steve and Jane, the two Americans they had met in Canopy Tower. And there they were, both of them with their binoculars in hand and both of them observing birds in Canopy Lodge's gardens. Daniel had now brought his two charges back to the lodge and they would now be able to fix to eat with this pair this evening and to catch up with what they had been doing since their time together at the Tower. Meanwhile, however, there was a lunch to have with their two drinking buddies, Kathy and Mary. And as these buddies were due to leave directly after lunch, Brian decided it should be a lunch to remember.

So eager was he to achieve this end that, after the event, he again couldn't remember a great deal about it, but he did remember talking about the different meaning of words in America and in the UK. He explained how these differences had first come to his attention when he'd spent a couple of months working in New York, just after the Ice Age back in 1976, and the very first example of these differences came to light when in an office one day he'd enquired whether anyone had a rubber. He, of course, had simply wanted to rub out something he'd written in pencil and not to equip himself with something one puts on one's 'pencil', but he had just not thought of the word 'eraser'. Similar embarrassments ensued from his ignorance of the different meaning of 'pants' on either side of the Atlantic, but the *pièce de résistance* in this divergence in one common language related to the use of the word 'fanny'.

In retrospect, Brian could not believe that he'd actually discussed the back-versus-front use of this word on either side of the Atlantic, but apparently he had – in some detail and much to the annoyance of his wife. His only defence was that he knew very well that Sandra revelled in all aspects of etymology and, more to the point, he was just very keen to unburden himself. That is to say, he was thoroughly loaded…

Anyway, lunch eventually came to an end, and after some heartfelt goodbyes, Kathy and Mary left the lodge and Brian and Sandra left the now even wetter outside world for a deserved rest in their room. And before any time at all, they were back in the restaurant and preparing to have dinner with Steve and Jane. This, it transpired, would be a meal not filled with too much frivolity but with rather too much seriousness – all thanks to Brian.

It had started with a debate between the four diners about the annihilation of wildlife in the world and the indisputable role that humans were playing in the eradication of so many animals and plants and the extinction of so many animal and plant species. It then moved on to how the introduction of an invasive species can play such an important part in this combined eradication and extinction process. How, by introducing a foreign species either unintentionally or as a result of some thoughtless or reckless venture, we can really mess things up. It is almost inevitable that the introduced species, if it manages to establish itself, will then go on to affect native species – by eating them, by competing with them or by introducing pathogens and parasites that will either kill them directly or by screwing up their habitat. And so Bob's your uncle. Another successful assault on the world's precious fauna – and flora – courtesy of thoughtless mankind.

Well, this was all fairly depressing but not in the least controversial and in no way politically incorrect. But that was before Brian decided to draw a parallel between the introduction of invasive species in the natural world and the current movement of humanity in the world of humans. They were two entirely different things, he conceded at the outset of his sermon, but at the same time they had so much in common.

Consider, he suggested, the arrival of the white Caucasian 'species' in the Americas and Australasia and the impact they had on the native 'species' that they found there. Because it was undeniable that if they didn't simply displace or enslave these native folks, then they went on to kill them, either directly or by donating them pathogens with which they just couldn't deal. The white wave clearly had all the hallmarks of a devastating invasive species.

Here Brian paused in his address, because he was just about to get not just mildly politically incorrect, but hugely politically incorrect – by discussing what is now happening to the 'white wave', both in its original European home and in its adopted homes in places such as the US, Australia and Canada. Quite simply, he suggested, it has given up its role as an invasive species and is itself being invaded by a new invasive species. That was not, he stressed, to be interpreted as a racist observation (although to those who have practised the art of taking offence at anything at all, it will be) but merely as a statement of fact. In an ever more overcrowded world, where white Caucasian birth rates have dipped and where those of other human races have not – leading to resource depletion and every other sort of problem in their home countries – it would be fanciful to believe that these 'others' wouldn't increasingly take on the role of an invasive species in those parts of the world that looked more attractive. That is to say, in those parts of the world housing white folks.

And that is exactly what was happening, pronounced Brian. The white Caucasian provinces all around the world were having to accommodate more and more 'introduced species' and as a result the 'native species' were being if not displaced then at least threatened by the prospect of being overwhelmed. Some of the principal practitioners of the process of introducing foreign species into the wrong environment – in the natural world – were now becoming the victims of a similar process in play in the exclusively human world. And there was, he suggested, no way to stop it. In short, he concluded, he and his three dinner companions would witness over the coming years not the death of their race, but its replacement or dilution by every other race on Earth, and whatever the political correctness brigade might say, nothing would stand in the way of that absolute certainty. Unless, of course, mankind as a whole managed to wipe itself out before the process was concluded...

At this point, there was a studied silence, as the recipients of Brian's message digested it as best they could. And only after a few seconds did Steve admit that he was in agreement with Brian – as would subsequently be admitted by Jane and Sandra as well – and then go on to wonder out loud whether he and his kind might ultimately be the recipients of the same sort of measures previously introduced to protect the Aboriginal people of Australia and the Native Americans of North America. Maybe there would be a programme of setting up tribal lands, places to where the overwhelmed whites could retreat and pursue some of their traditional pastimes, such as drinking beer, playing baseball (or rugby), watching TV and ignoring the increasingly harsh reality of a world in distress.

There was no consensus on what would happen in terms of protective measures, but Brian did express the hope that there would not be a need to resort to captive breeding programmes. At which point the entire introduced-species debate concluded, and all four diners were soon on their way to their rooms. It had been a fun-filled, birdy-filled day for them all, and for two of them there was still a little fun to come. Brian still had to present his evening entertainment…

Tonight it was to be a discourse on budgerigars in cages. And Brian had decided to kick off proceedings by reminding his wife of the ubiquity of these caged seed-eating parrots. He would then explain to her how they were a common, almost required, feature of so many homes in fifties and sixties Britain. Then he would probably go on to opine that it was a bloody good thing that the caging of any birds was now well out of fashion, at least in that threatened white world discussed over dinner. However, things did not go to plan. As soon as he'd announced his theme, Sandra asked him whether budgie-smugglers really did get their name from their appearance – as in the similarity between a bulge caused by a gentleman's genitals and one resulting from the housing of contraband birdlife of the budgerigar variety in close-fitting swimwear.

Well, that did it. Brian was able to confirm that this is exactly how they came by their name, but the bubble had been burst. He no longer wanted to talk about caged as opposed to secreted budgies, and he was fairly sure that Sandra wanted to hear no such chat. So he pursued it no further and resigned himself to some much-needed sleep. And to get himself to sleep, he decided to search his memory to discover whether he had ever owned anything pink. He knew he had never owned a pink steering-wheel cover, and certainly never a shocking-pink contraceptive – but maybe there had been something. Yes! Maybe… maybe, years and years ago, in the family home, there might well have been a pink budgerigar…

7.

arlos was a jerk. Brian knew this the moment he set eyes on him. He just had that look about him, that look that says 'I am a jerk'. So it was no great surprise that he behaved like a jerk – as, of course, any genuine jerk would. Sandra soon picked up on it too. Only seconds after meeting his new clients, he was just far too friendly, far too inquisitive and *far, far* too self-assured. He could have been no more than thirty, but he was one of the most accomplished jerks that Brian had ever had the misfortune to meet (and he'd met a lot in his time).

He was, it should be explained, the driver of Brian and Sandra's transfer vehicle that would take them back to Panama City. Because today they would be travelling to the far north-west of Panama, and that would involve a car journey into Panama City, followed by a flight to a place on the Caribbean coast called Bocas Del Toro. This, of course, meant that just after breakfast they had to say their goodbyes to Steve and Jane – and then they had to put themselves in the hands of a jerk for the two-hour ride back to Panama City. And, thanks to Carlos's accomplished-jerk status, this proved to be just as bad an experience as Brian had feared, if not worse.

It started with a short drive into El Valle de Antón and then a much longer drive along the steep, winding road that led back to the miserable Pan-American Highway. The short drive wasn't too bad. Carlos had little time to pick up speed and he was already beginning to run out of questions. But the longer drive on the other side of El Valle de Antón was a different matter altogether. Within a very short time indeed it illustrated that Carlos the Jerk didn't really know how to drive a car. In the first place, he drove too quickly – full stop. And in the second place, he had simply no idea of how to take bends, which, given that the steep road back to the highway was just a series of bends, was a little disconcerting for his passengers. He was repeatedly having to take corrective action at the last second to keep his vehicle on the road or to prevent it from coming into contact with another vehicle. In fact, Brian soon formed the impression that not only could this guy not drive, but he also could not learn from his repeated mistakes. He could not see that if he drove more slowly – and stopped accelerating towards bends – he wouldn't continually be having to make corrections to his driving. In short, he appeared to have no common sense.

Matters improved a little when Brian informed him that they had more than enough time to check in for their flight in the early afternoon, and therefore it would be greatly appreciated if he didn't drive so effin' fast… However, there was nothing Brian could do to overcome his lack of common sense, which manifested itself in quite a different way on the litter-edged Pan-American Highway.

This dual carriageway road operates on the normal slow-lane/overtaking-lane principle found on most two-lane dual carriageways in the world. Indeed, at regular intervals along the highway are little signs reminding Panama's drivers that this is the way that the road should be used. Unfortunately, however, it is used in this way by only about half of Panama's drivers, while the other half have opted for the alternative approach. That is to say, they use the overtaking lane as the slow lane, and use the real slow lane only if they want to undertake another of their sort that is blocking their way. The result is a combination of frustration, alarm and just pure nonsense. It completely lacks common sense.

No prizes then for guessing which approach was adopted by Carlos – in a car that could speed down winding roads but that could barely maintain forward motion when asked to tackle upward inclines on the P-A Highway.

He never left the overtaking lane once, and through this display of the antithesis of common sense he caused countless faster cars to undertake him – when he wasn't just causing a rolling road block by driving at the same speed as a vehicle on the inside lane to his right. He didn't even pull over when he negotiated a couple of long, down-gradient curves in the highway, when anyone with an iota of common sense and just a fragile grasp of the actions of centrifugal force would have immediately concluded that life in that empty lane on the right would be just that much easier – and not quite so alarming for his passengers.

To say Brian and Sandra were extremely relieved when they reached the airport would not be an overstatement.

In fact, they were elated, even though Carlos had left them to negotiate the airport's check-in procedures on their own. And that might prove a challenge. This wasn't Tocumen International Airport, but the much smaller Albrook 'International' Airport, a facility that in its former life had been a US Airforce base and that in its present life didn't seem too concerned with stuff such as signage or useful passenger information. So it was just a case of trial and error, which in the end did deliver Brian and Sandra into a departure lounge, and with boarding cards for the correct Air Panama flight. Here, while they waited, Brian began to think that a lack of common sense might become the theme of the day. After all, women wearing skin-tight clothes in the humid heat of Panama just didn't make any sense at all. But that's what they all did (whether they were just ten stone or twice this weight). And then there was the hour's delay (for a half-hour flight) while the aeroplane's crew waited for a second stewardess to turn up who, on the flight itself, would do no more than the other stewardess did – which was nothing. No food was served. No drinks were served. And the passengers on the plane weren't even treated to a smile.

Anyway, the plane eventually landed in Bocas Del Toro 'International' Airport, essentially a short, single runway providing unedifying views of the filth of Bocas Del Toro town and yet another manifestation of the lack of common sense in this country. This time it was in respect of the baggage reclaim arrangements. These first involved the unloading of the baggage from the arriving plane onto a couple of waiting baggage carts – in plain view of Brian and Sandra and another one hundred or so poor saps who had been herded into the scruffy terminal building. Then, following on from this first step, was the loading of the baggage for the outward flight onto the same plane – while the inward baggage was simply ignored. And only when that loading had been completed was any thought given to reuniting the landed baggage with its now restless owners. This was achieved by sliding the bags, one at a time, into the terminal building where, within a scrum of people, one was then required to identify one's own luggage and to retrieve it only after one had produced one's baggage tag. It was, of course, a recipe for pandemonium, and in all the airports Brian and Sandra had visited over the years, they had never witnessed a baggage reclaim system that was so devoid of common sense. Perhaps things would improve when they left the airport…

Well, they did, but only a little. They had been shown to a minibus – which was soon packed with other travellers – and this bus then began its very short journey into downtown Bocas Del Toro. This was a cross between a frontier town in the American Wild West and somewhere not quite so salubrious. It was a complete mess, and when Brian and Sandra were deposited in its main thoroughfare, they began to wonder what they had let themselves in for.

They need not have worried – at least about the state of Bocas Del Toro. Because they were immediately taken through a restaurant by their guide (?) and onto a wharf at its rear. And there it was, their new source of concern: a small, open boat that would take them to their next lodge – which was on an island and more than fifteen miles away. Oh, and it was already raining a little and the colour of the sky indicated that it would soon be raining a great deal more.

Their guide-cum-boat-driver could clearly see there was a threat of increased precipitation. Because as soon as Brian and Sandra had boarded the boat, he found a couple of XXL bin liners and into these he put their two bags. They would now remain dry no matter how hard it rained. Unfortunately, he had no similar bin liners for his two passengers, and there was no doubt about it; they would not remain dry at all. Indeed, even in their waterproof tops, they were in for a soaking. There was simply no shelter on the motor-powered boat – other than a minute canopy over the control console for the benefit of their driver – so that when the rain began to fall in earnest they began to get drenched. And at the end of the forty-minute open-boat transfer to their destination they were completely saturated. Sandra was not happy and Brian just felt dismayed. Heck, he thought, what did a transfer like this say about where they had just arrived: the establishment that was responsible for this transfer and that called itself the Tranquilo Bay Eco Adventure Lodge? Was the method adopted to receive its guests all part of its eco-adventure credentials – and if so, would Brian and Sandra now find themselves having to pitch a tent?

Well, no. On the contrary, they were immediately whisked off to a beautifully appointed cabin nestling within some lush vegetation, and containing within it a generous store of much-needed towels. Furthermore,

Jim, one of the co-owners of the lodge who had done the whisking, then offered to take Brian's jeans to the lodge's laundry in order to dry them in time for dinner. And before then, he asked, would his two new guests like some mildly intoxicating refreshment to aid the process of settling in? He would arrange for it to be brought to their cabin.

Brian's mood changed immediately and Sandra's did as soon as she'd had a shower and her first sip of beer. The Tranquilo Bay Eco Adventure Lodge was showing all sorts of promise – and even though it was now getting dark, it was crystal clear that Brian and Sandra had landed somewhere that bore no relationship whatsoever to the rough and ready shabbiness of Bocas Del Toro town. They were in another world, and a world that contained a first-floor bar-cum-lounge-cum-dining-room in the main lodge building, and that at 7.00 required their attendance for further refreshment.

They made it there with the help of an umbrella (it was still raining), and as soon as they arrived, they met the only other guests who were staying in the lodge, an American couple called Jay and James and a Canadian couple called Linda and Wayne. All proved good company over dinner, and Linda and Wayne were of particular interest as it was soon established that their itinerary would again cross that of Brian and Sandra's in just a few days' time. And that was very welcome news. They were both particularly interesting and, as far as Brian could tell, they were not too appalled by his own twisted views or his own twisted sense of humour. There again, he had attempted to show some restraint on this, their first evening together, and had saved his most contorted idea – if not his warped sense of humour – for Sandra's evening entertainment. This became evident when, back in their room, he treated Sandra to her latest dose of 'what has gone from our lives' – which this evening was 'police'.

'We never see them anymore,' he began. 'Sixty years ago, they were all over the place, and your chances of making it back home from the flicks – on a bike with a faulty back light – were zero. Somewhere or other there'd be a PC Plod who would step out of the shadows and nab you. And woe betide you if he caught you again. Whereas now… well, they're all back at the police station, investigating the latest hate crime on social media or safeguarding the human rights of a gang of toerags in the cells. Or maybe they're even locked away in a room investigating an "historic" crime committed fifty years ago, which has got about as much chance of getting to court in the next fifty years as I've got of getting to the moon. Meanwhile, the muggers and the burglars and the car-jackers all have a field day. Not only do they know that there are just not enough police out and about to catch them, but even if they are exceptionally unlucky and they do get caught, they will receive only a slap on the wrist. You see…'

'Brian,' interrupted Sandra sharply, 'I do not believe you can put the police into the same category as… antimacassars and suspenders. And even if you want to, all I want is to get some sleep. And I…'

'I've nearly finished,' re-interrupted Brian. 'And all I was going to say is that if one looks back – to a time in Britain when there wasn't a police force – some sort of order was kept by imposing draconian penalties on transgressors. They were made to know that they might well get away with their misdeeds, but if they didn't, they might well lose their life or they might at least have to learn how to defend themselves against marauding kangaroos…'

'Brian!'

'Anyway, we then developed a police force, and the deterrent switched from draconian penalties to the much-increased likelihood of being caught. Sheep stealers were no longer hanged and interfering with sheep was no longer an automatic ticket to the Antipodes. Penalties became – and still are – soft.'

'And?' encouraged Sandra.

'They shouldn't be. We are now getting back to that time when, with so few police available to catch criminals, the criminals need to be deterred by some extremely severe punishments.'

'Hanging and deportation again!?' squawked Sandra.

'No. There'd be too many problems with liberals and Aussies. I was thinking more of the standard internment stuff we do now, but with a continuous soundtrack.'

'Eh?'

'You incarcerate a villain and expose him to a constant twenty-four-hour diet of… well, let's say the proceedings of the House of Lords, the collected recordings of speeches by Neil Kinnock and Gordon Brown and every football report that's been played on regional news programmes for the last forty years. And I can guarantee that the likelihood of that villain ever getting himself locked up again will be as near as damn it to zero, and lots of other villains who haven't yet been caught will quickly change their ways. That sort of incarceration will be a *real* deterrent and far more of a deterrent than the current arrangements which seem to be on a par with a spell in a Premier Inn – if not better than a spell in a Premier Inn…'

'Premier Inns are very nice.'

'My point exactly.'

Sandra huffed, and then she made what would prove to be her final observation for the evening.

'Brian,' she started, 'I think your idea is complete nonsense – of course – but you might have given it a little more credibility if you'd scrubbed the contributions by Messrs Kinnock and Brown and instead proposed the collected recordings of… Brian the Oracle – as delivered over forty years to his longsuffering wife.'

She said this with a glint in her eye, but it had the desired effect. Brian closed down for the night and now gave some further thought to the dearth of common sense in Panama. And was the provision of an open boat to transfer guests in a frequent-rain environment a further example of this dearth which he had failed to spot at the time? Yes, he decided, it was.

Though not such an obvious example as sitting in the wrong bloody lane on a dual carriageway…

8.

For Brian, the night had been undisturbed. Unfortunately, however, the same could not be said for his breakfast.

It was all down to his and Sandra's designated guide, the guy who would be at their disposal for their entire stay at Tranquilo Bay and who introduced himself as Ramon. That for Brian – and Sandra – would have been quite enough: his simply introducing himself and his then retiring to allow them to relish their first meal of the day in peace. After all, for both of them, breakfast had never been a particularly sociable meal, and for Brian, the idea of a 'working breakfast' had been up there with open-plan offices and unisex loos as one of the reasons he'd been so relieved to have quit the world of work. Hell, conversations over breakfast, as far as he was concerned, should be restricted to a debate on the whereabouts of the jam and the need for another round of toast. They should certainly not extend to a dissertation on the myriad activity options available to guests of the lodge, and certainly not while they were still trying to establish what the options were for the elements of their breakfast. How could Brian even choose what fruit juice he wanted when he was being assailed with an avalanche of information from Ramon, most of which was either irrelevant or unintelligible? (Ramon was Spanish and he spoke both rapidly and indistinctly.) The result, for both Brian and his wife, was a fraught feeding experience and a growing apprehension of what two days with a loquacious Spaniard might mean for their stay at the lodge. Would they end up having to hide from Ramon?

Well, for the moment that was neither necessary nor practical. They very much wanted to explore the grounds of the lodge in search of birds, and whatever else Ramon was, he was certainly a good bird guide. They had been told so the previous evening. So, although it was still trying to rain after breakfast, Brian and Sandra willingly put themselves in the hands of their very personal guide and embarked on a morning's birding walk to savour whatever local delights they could discover.

It should be explained at this point that the Tranquilo Bay lodge is situated on Isla Bastimentos, an island on the Caribbean side of Panama, extending to an area of twenty square miles. The island is mostly forested and it has no roads, no cars and not even an airstrip. It has not yet been *developed*. Happily, Tranquilo Bay has been constructed to recognise the pristine nature of this unspoilt location and its footprint is a light one. Its main building, its small number of *cabanas* and its staff accommodation are all modest and they sit within 200 heavily forested acres of the island, a beautiful patch of land that is bordered by almost a kilometre of Caribbean coastline. It is a wonderful place to visit and a wonderful place to see birds.

This was proved beyond doubt within minutes of the group of three setting off. The immediate grounds of the lodge offered a mix of forest and more open areas, and all around there were birds of all sorts. Brian found it difficult to take them all in, but he would remember for quite some time two in particular. One was a splendid boat-billed flycatcher, which is a large tyrant flycatcher that must feature in the nightmares of many a fly. And the other was a striking red-capped manakin who was having a bath. Brian liked to think he was smartening himself up for a bit of courting, which for a male red-capped manakin involves him shuffling rapidly backwards across a branch, in a manner that has been likened to a speedy moonwalk. That display was not on offer today – possibly because that threat of rain had soon turned into actual rain.

This couldn't be ignored. Neither could the intense humidity, the discomfort of wearing a waterproof in intense humidity, nor the copious amounts of mud underfoot that threatened to upend the birders at every step. Neither could the two amateur birders ignore Ramon. He was proving just as verbose as they had feared and they soon came to believe that he probably kept on talking whether he had an audience or not, and that there was even the probability that his sleeping hours were filled with yet more endless chatter. Talking for Ramon was no different to breathing. It's just what you did all the time – without a break, without a thought and particularly without thinking what its impact might be on others, especially if they could make out only a little of what you were saying.

Brian and Sandra couldn't decide what was better: the shower they had when they got back to their cabin or the cabin itself, which guaranteed them at least a temporary respite from Ramon's verbal attentions. In the end they decided that it was the cabin itself. After that they decided that the cheese and meat baps that were presented for lunch could have won a prize for being the most daunting baps ever designed for human consumption, along with an honourable mention in the 'most unappetising' category. They were awful, but unfortunately not that out of keeping with the other meals at the lodge (last night's had been quite grim and those to come would be no better).

On a more positive note, the afternoon consisted of a well-deserved spell of indolence back at the cabin and then what would constitute quite literally the highpoint of the day: a visit to the top of the lodge's observation tower.

This was different from the observation tower in the Soberania National Park – and it had certainly not required the services of a tower designer in its construction. Instead the owners of the lodge had purchased a couple of obsolete cell-phone masts in the States, had shipped them to Bocas Del Toro and then somehow to their present location – and then erected them to form the basic structure of the tower. Clearly there was some additional work required to provide this basic structure with stuff like steps and a handrail, but essentially anyone climbing this 100-foot column was entrusting his or her life to the hardware spawned by the iPhone wave. And pretty insubstantial hardware at that...

Nevertheless, Brian and Sandra were not deterred by the fragile-looking nature of the tower and were soon climbing up to its rather exposed observation deck where they met up with Ramon and Wayne. It wobbled only a little bit, and Brian was soon able to ignore the wobble and begin to take in the view. It was of a large slice of Isla Bastimentos and its mangrove-covered fringes and it was sublime. It more than confirmed that this place, with its virtually unbroken carpet of trees, was a very special place indeed, and inevitably just as fragile if not more so than the observation tower itself. Commercial Bocas Del Toro was just too close for comfort, and at some point it would inevitably take an interest in its 'neighbour across the way'. The developers would recognise the island's potential – if they hadn't done so already – and Isla Bastimentos would come under siege.

Anyway, for the moment it was still sublime, and it clearly hosted a healthy population of birds, many of which could be observed with ease from the top of the tower. Ramon was pointing them all out. And taking account of the 360-degree field of view, there being lots of birds around and Ramon having an enviable ability to spot them, this meant that he was pointing them out more or less constantly. He certainly wasn't going to abandon his habit of ceaseless chatter if he could help it, and in this instance Brian couldn't really complain. Without Ramon, he, Sandra and Wayne would have seen or identified only a fraction of the birds that they did. And Brian might even have been unable to ignore the ever-present wobbles, which, with the arrival of three more guests onto the observation deck, had now become significantly bigger wobbles and really quite unnerving.

Needless to say, however, a controlled rather than a dramatic descent of the tower was achieved by the whole party, and in due course all the lodge's guests turned up for dinner. Brian and Sandra shared theirs with Jim's wife, Rene, and Linda and Wayne, and it was Rene who initially led the conversation by confirming Brian's worst fears about the fragility of any of the local unspoilt environment. She informed her guests that whilst the majority of Isla Bastimentos, along with some other smaller islands, was within a defined national park, 'the balance between conservation and development was tipping in favour of the latter'. Indifferent or corrupt government officials, she said, were doing little to stop this tilting towards doom, and the agencies they worked for were grossly underfunded. That was why, she went on, the Panamanian section of the huge La Amistad International Park, which spans the Panamanian and Costa Rican border and which falls mostly within the Bocas Del Toro province, lacked any real protection. There were, apparently, only a handful of rangers to guard the 400,000 hectares on the Panamanian side. Conservation, she emphasised, was not high on the agenda of an administration based in faraway Panama City – and which could see all sorts of short-term gains in adopting a 'develop and be damned' approach in so many parts of the country.

Well, this was all getting pretty depressing, which is why Brian thought it was about time that he steered the conversation in a completely different direction. The degradation of the natural environment was appalling but it was difficult to see how, in Panama, it could be arrested. So, why not turn to something of a little less importance but something to which there might be a solution, namely the current polarisation of so many Western democracies…

It was indisputable, Brian contended, that certain modern democracies were experiencing unprecedented divisions in their electorates, with voters on each side of the divide holding contradictory and seemingly irreconcilable views. In the United States, for example, the Republicans were locked in a vicious battle with the Democrats, and in Britain there was a sharper divide than ever between those of its voters who have experienced the devastating impact of full-blown socialism and those who have not (or who have chosen to forget it). And it was difficult, he suggested, to see how this degree of polarity wouldn't at some point undermine the very existence of these democracies. Something would have to give, and it would probably be the operation of representative democracy as we know it today. Unless, of course, the polarised populations took a radically different route. Unless, as Brian revealed, they accepted that they would probably be better off apart – physically.

Brian's audience looked a little nonplussed at this stage, but as soon as he went on to explain what this physical separation would be, they looked more nonplussed than ever. Because what he was suggesting was the physical relocation of huge tranches of both countries' populations, and then the constitution in each country of two brand-new sovereign states. That is to say that in America, there would be a Democratic US – occupying a horseshoe-shaped country made up of the existing West Coast and East Coast states with a wide corridor just below the Canadian border joining the two – and a Republican US occupying the middle and south of the country. Likewise in England, the rational half of the population would be given the north and the west of the country, while the brave new socialists would be awarded London and the South East (which they would find difficult to make any worse than they already were).

This might sound a rather radical approach, conceded Brian, but the end result of these possibly painful upheavals would be the creation of four new countries with truly coherent populations in terms of their outlook and values, and the ability to maintain this coherence by offering those who realised they were in the wrong camp the opportunity to migrate to the right camp. After all, he suggested, it wouldn't be too long before the attractions of life in the Democratic US or in the north and west of England became apparent to many of those on the other side of the respective borders, and the resulting shift in political allegiances would be like nothing ever witnessed before.

Well, nobody actually said that Brian was talking out of an alternative orifice, but Wayne did make the observation that if Brian held a university degree, he would wager with anyone that it was not in political science. Although it might have been better for all concerned if it was.

Brian was not in the least offended. He knew that there were many great thinkers through the ages who had not been recognised as great thinkers in their own time. Only when they had passed on was their genius acknowledged and their ideas accepted for what they were: brilliant but a little before their time.

In fact, strangely enough, the premature nature of his thinking would again become evident when, back in their room, he treated Sandra to her latest dose of 'what has gone from our lives', which this evening was 'bob-a-job week'. He started his latest assault with a question.

'Do you remember bob-a-job week? You know, all those Scouts turning up on your doorstep offering to do more or less anything for just a shilling.'

Sandra looked surprisingly engaged and for once she responded to Brian's question with a noticeable amount of enthusiasm.

'Yes,' she said, 'I do. Or at least I remember the idea of bob-a-job week. I can't remember ever getting an actual Scout on my doorstep…'

'No. Neither can I,' replied Brian. 'But I think I did some bob-a-jobbing when I was a Scout myself. You know, mowing a lawn or weeding a flower bed or something like that. A little bit of harmless slave labour that nobody seemed to mind…'

'What happened to it?'

'Errh… health and safety laws, compensation claims, the fear of paedophiles. You know. All the various sorts of bollocks that gets in the way anything these days. Even slave labour.'

'Oh.'

'Yeah, they ditched it in the 1990s sometime. And all that exists now is some sort of *community* stuff. You know, organised – and adult supervised – stuff, which isn't quite the same as letting some youngster loose on yer lawn edges. And God knows what Baden Powell would have made of it. Not quite in the traditions of teaching young sprots how to be independent and self-reliant.'

'That probably ranks as child abuse these days.'

'Yeah, it probably does. And it's all the more sad, because there are just so many little jobs these days that would be perfect for a modern Scout. And I don't know why that Chief Scout of theirs hasn't seen it.'

'Jobs such as?'

'Well, sorting out a non-functioning function key on your laptop; sorting out how to do that cut and paste thing without screwing everything up – or how to reinstate that stuff you deleted by mistake.'

'You mean, they could act as sort of computing consultants?'

'Yep. They'll have all the skills that a lot of oldies like us don't have – and they could even apply these skills remotely. You know, through that TeamViewer thing. So no problems with "safeguarding issues" and there wouldn't even be any accidents with shears. It'd be perfect.'

Sandra didn't look convinced, and Brian could see this. He knew his proposal was yet another that fell into the 'brilliant but before its time' category, and that it would be rejected like so many others. Even if the stakes were raised and bob-a-job week became known as 'quid-pro-quo' week (or would that have to be five-quid-pro-quo week?).

Yes, it was time to abandon his ideas for a revival in the Scouts' financial fortunes and lull himself to sleep with thoughts of how he now had ahead of him nine hours of Ramon-free time, nine hours without that continuous if well-meant soundtrack.

Oh, and nine hours of not having to test his overworked genius...

9.

rian was rarely up at 6.45 in the morning. He was almost never up 100-foot in the air at this time in the morning. Indeed, such an early exercise in elevation was more or less unheard of. However, on this new Tranquilo Bay morning, it had happened. Without even a mouthful of muesli to sustain him, he had joined Sandra in an early-morning ascent of the observation tower to expose himself to Ramon's logorrhoea (your new word for the day – look it up) and, more appealingly, to Tranquilo Bay's early morning birds.

They were around in numbers, and some of them were very special. There were, for example, some green ibises flying by – and a tricoloured heron, a beautiful black-cheeked woodpecker and a variable seedeater, looking, on this wonderful sunny morning, rather more constant in his appearance than variable. In fact, he looked no more variable than the sloth who was encountered as Ramon and his two charges descended the tower, although maybe marginally more active. Like all other sloths in the world, this sloth looked as though he had all the time in the world – to do nothing – and he once again reinforced Brian's admiration for these animals, creatures who had synchronised their pace of life to that of the forest and who, by doing so, had achieved the title of 'the most laid-back critters on Earth' – in their style as well as in their physical disposition.

Any sort of laid-back had, of course, alluded Ramon – by a mile. He wasn't so much easy-going as difficult to come to terms with, especially over breakfast. A session of loquacity on the tower had not drained him of his talkativeness and, having insisted on again joining Brian and Sandra for their first meal of the day, he ensured that not a second of it was spent in silence. This guy, thought Brian, with his incessant intended-to-be-informative prose, could, all on his own, be the cause of a really bad case of post-didactic stress disorder, and Brian was relieved beyond words that he and Sandra had to share his company for just one further day. He was a really nice chap – sort of – but he just didn't know when to put a sock in it, and accordingly 'it' was always open and spewing out words in an endless procession. If he was remunerated on the basis of his word count, thought Brian, he would be wealthier than Philip Green. Although, of course, nowhere near as unpleasant.

Anyway, breakfast was finally concluded, and it was time for another ground-level birding session with Ramon. This one took in a different part of the forest and, solely due to the skill of their much-maligned guide, one of the most remarkable 'bird-shows' that Brian and Sandra had ever encountered. It was where a tiny stream ran through the forest (and where there were several mosquitoes about) and it involved a remarkable performance by three species of hummingbirds. It was their bathing spot, and as Ramon and his two transfixed visitors stood and gazed, one sort of hummingbird after another would come to perform their mid-morning ablutions. First of all, it was a crowned woodnymph, a sparkling green and blue gem with small wings. Then it was a purple-crowned fairy – not a delicate sprite with magical powers, but a delicate bird with magical looks. And then finally a stripe-throated hermit, a hummingbird weighing no more than three grams, which is in no way reclusive but which instead tends to be more noticeably vocal than most other species of hummingbirds. But what really made the appearance of these three birds so special was their choosing to bathe in the stream – only feet from where their observers were standing – and for their each choosing a different way to bathe. One seemed to prefer the hesitate-then-plunge approach, one the more considered and careful approach, and the third the repeated dainty-dip approach. It was quite fascinating and for Brian and Sandra a vivid reminder of why they were prepared to trudge around a muddy forest in intense humidity – and with a well-meaning guide who came without even a pause button, let alone an off switch. Oh, and that wasn't all. Ramon even found for them some red poison-dart frogs, which apparently produce toxins which can affect a human's nervous system, but unfortunately not the operation of its sometimes-overworked vocal chords...

Yes, Ramon was still at it over lunch, but at least the overused wildlife soundtrack had been replaced by one that dealt with politics, and specifically the politics of Spain. This started by Ramon's informing Brian and

Sandra that, although Spanish by birth, he had decided to spend his life in Panama (with his Colombian wife) not only because of the natural environment of the country but also because he detested what was happening in his native land. It was, he explained very forcefully, not a real democracy but a fascist state masquerading as a democracy, a place where Franco's legacy was still very much alive and where this legacy was ensuring that malevolence and bitterness were at the heart of its increasingly confrontational society.

He told his guests that he had it on good authority from some of his relatives back home that when the (national) Civil Guard and the National Police Corps used excessive violence to put down protests in Catalonia in 2017, they received a great deal of encouragement to do this. And this encouragement came in the form of residents in their (non-Catalan) home towns exhorting them, as they went off to Catalonia, to 'put the boot in to those upstart Catalans' to teach them who was still in charge of this country (presumably, the followers of somebody who rhymes with Blanco boot polish – if one ignores the boot polish). And whether Ramon was entirely accurate in his assessment of Spain and whether these stories about the degree of hatred for the Catalans were entirely true, one could not ignore the reality of the brutality shown by the national police, nor the enduring divisions in that country ever since it was run by the Blanco kid. There was something wrong in Spain, and it had taken a trip to the north-west of Panama for this to be confirmed by one of that country's sons. And he did seem entirely credible.

Wow! Well, Brian would not easily forget that lunch, but there was now an afternoon to deal with – and Brian and Sandra, one might recall, were in the Tranquilo Bay Eco *Adventure* Lodge. This wasn't a place that offered only bird-watching and nature walks, but also pursuits such as fishing, kayaking, snorkelling and surfing. Indeed, before they had left in the middle of the day, Linda and Wayne had made very good use of the lodge's kayaks, and Brian was sorely tempted to take to the water in one of these devices with, if possible, his wife in tow. There again, the snorkelling sounded very inviting. Or maybe it should be the turn of some invigorating surfing.

Well, Brian and Sandra, back in their cabana, tussled with these choices for quite some time, and right up until they were overtaken with an extended siesta. Brian blamed the early-morning start and the demanding all-morning hike. Sandra opted for the effects of Ramon's uninterrupted commentary combined with their advancing old age. But whatever the cause, 'adventure' was put on hold, and the only further activity that would be undertaken today would involve a dining table and the company of an English couple from Yorkshire.

The male of this couple, it was learned, had an inbuilt defibrillator and, as could be inferred from the over-dinner conversation, his wife did not. What both of them did have, however, was an ability to cope with Brian's latest thoughtful speculation, and this one stemmed from Ramon's earlier diatribe against his native Spain. He began it by providing them with a precis of what Ramon had said, how Spanish democracy was not really a democracy at all, but just a cloak used to conceal that country's essential authoritarianism, by those in the country who held the real power. He then went on to consider why, unlike most of the other countries in Europe, Spain had ended up in this somewhat dysfunctional situation, and he started by examining its early history, when it was busying itself with piling up wealth and possessions overseas. Was it, he pondered out loud, something to do with how it actually went about amassing these riches and what this meant for the citizens of the nations it looted? Hell, it wasn't as though the Spanish were too fussed about the impact of their actions, and their whole 'conquistador' approach was infused not just with indifference but with out and out brutality. Spain could quite easily have given colonialism the sort of bad name from which it would never recover…

Or there again, he wondered, was it those blasted English, those disagreeable bastards from the north, who were always too far south and far too bloody adept at pinching Spain's gold and making its life as a colonial power really rather tiresome and far less of a prize than it should have been? In fact, the English were just bad news in every way possible. If they weren't sinking Spanish galleons, they were sinking Spanish armadas and, possibly worse of all for modern Spain, they were making themselves very unwelcome as immediate neighbours. Yes, Brian suggested, maybe having Gibraltar at the foot of Spain is, for Spain, like having a piece of grit in your boot, and a piece of grit that eventually sends you mad. Like you develop a case of chronic fascism manifesting itself either as a faux democracy or, not that long ago, as an acute case of naked despotism.

By this stage of his musings, Brian was possibly losing his audience, but he then revealed that he doubted it was anything to do with Spain's history or the pernicious effect of the perfidious Brits. It wasn't even the favourable climate of Spain – which might be responsible for its fragile work ethic but which could never be found guilty of poisoning its very psyche. The real reason for this country's national disorder, he finally declared, was quite clearly down to its citizens' habit of eating their dinners at any time between 9.00 and 11.00 in the evening. This was quite preposterous, he maintained. It led to overnight discomfort, persistent insomnia, greatly impaired love-making capabilities, troublesome bowel activity – and a deep-seated affinity for fascism, either as a government or as the substance of a government.

At this point, the man with the defibrillator asked Brian what Spain might do to extricate itself from its unfortunate condition, if this was at all possible. Brian replied that it was indeed possible and the first and most important step it would have to take would be to introduce laws that made late-evening eating illegal. Meals would have to finish by 9.00, not start at this time (or even later). This, however, would not be enough. The Spanish, he declared, would also have to turn their bull-fighting arenas into cricket grounds. There was no clearer sign of Spain's malaise than its interest in disrespecting and dispatching bulls in such a callous manner. Similarly, there was no clearer sign of the operation of a genuine democracy (with a couple of notable exceptions) than its host country embracing cricket as its most civilised national game. Where the killing of bulls would stir passion in the hearts of men, five days of gentle sportsmanship would calm their souls and let them see that early eating is good and fascism is bad, if not very bad. And hey presto, within months Spain would join that community of nations that had a real, failing, unsustainable, under-threat representative democracy. And it might even qualify for the Cricket World Cup.

Well, Brian wasn't entirely sure that he'd really convinced his audience with his thoughtful analysis or his even more thoughtful prescription for Spain's chronic ills. So he wrapped up proceedings with a couple of his homemade Trump witticisms. The first was: 'What's the difference between a Russian puppet and an American President?' – to which the answer was 'nothing'. And the second was that a good codename for a Russian spy would be 'Ivan knows all', which could be abbreviated for convenience to 'Ivanka'.

It was no good. He was flogging a dead horse. It was time to return to the matrimonial cabana and regale his matrimonial partner with her next 'what has disappeared' entertainment. And tonight, what would be disinterred from the past was the paternoster lift…

'Did you know,' he started 'that the construction of paternoster lifts in the UK was stopped as far back as the mid-1970s – for safety reasons?'

'No,' replied Sandra.

'You know what I mean, don't you? Those things that had a sort of chain of open compartments that moved up and down a building in a loop and without stopping. You just had to step into it – and then out of it.'

'Yeah, there was one at my college in Brum. It was really good. No waiting and no problems.'

'Well, somebody thought there were problems, which is why they were effectively banned, and you now have only a couple that survive in the UK. And I'm pretty sure they'll soon be gone as well.'

'What sort of problems?'

'Oh, you know, the odd death. That sort of thing. And all blown out of proportion of course. Like the odd one or two deaths in a trillion always is.'

'So, I might never see one again?'

'Well, maybe. If my idea gets taken up by a few universities…'

'What!?'

'Well, a lot of these paternosters were in colleges and universities, weren't they? And that's where they should be reinstalled.'

'What for?'

'Well, to start with they represent a very efficient way of delivering students to their chosen destination. And what's more, something that requires a little concentration and agility might not be a bad thing for that huge army of snowflakes. You know, that horde of precious little darlings who seem incapable of tearing their attention away from their screens.'

'Oh, I see.'

'Yes, and my idea also includes a "rapid transit" paternoster, a lift that would travel at twice the normal speed, and through an electronic-tagging regime would be the obligatory means of transport for all those really stupid students. You know, all those absolute idiots who want to impose their imbecilic, puritan ideology on everybody else and those other morons who can't help judging the actions of others in the past by their own ignorant and witless standards of the present – which presuppose that they have reached some sort of nirvana of standards that won't itself fall foul of judgements made in the future. Well, a good bit of terror-in-transit might just drill some sense into them. I mean, hell, it must be worth a try…'

Sandra looked tired.

'Brian,' she said, 'I sometimes wish you took medication. 'Cos if you did, I might be able to ask you whether you'd forgotten to take it. Like now, for example.'

Oh well, he couldn't win them all. Although, there again, it would be nice to win one occasionally.

Or even just one…

10.

It was time to leave Tranquilo Bay, and that meant time, once again, to board a small open boat. Fortunately, however, on this occasion the sky was blue and there was little chance that Brian and Sandra would experience the sort of soaking they'd had three days before. Instead there was just the prospect of an early-morning ride to the Panamanian mainland in the company of a boatman who had little English and little interest in maintaining a modest speed. Soon after setting off, he absolutely raced along – and turned what could have been a leisurely hour-long transfer into one lasting barely forty minutes. This was a pity in a way, because his route took him past the mostly uninhabited coastlines of a couple of small islands and then into the Laguna de Chiriqui, a beautiful, largely unspoilt lagoon that was as empty as it was handsome. Which is more than could be said for Punta Róbalo…

This is where Brian and Sandra were landed, a 'town' on the edge of the lagoon whose greatest asset was that it had a road that led out of it. Its tiny jetty was in a state of collapse, its twenty or so houses were hovering somewhere between decrepit and entirely derelict, and its visible population (of two people) looked as clapped out as the settlement itself. It was in a wonderful situation but a dreadful condition, and Brian could not help feeling that it had suffered years of neglect and was now suffering from a really bad case of dejection and despair. Punta Róbalo was not a happy place to be.

Brian and Sandra both felt mildly uncomfortable as they waited in what might once have been the town's open-sided market, but which was now just a covered space with a couple of breezeblocks to sit on. And that cover was needed. The sun was now getting very strong and, through hand gestures, their boatman had insisted they took shelter from it in this dilapidated edifice while they waited for their onward transfer. Because today, the boat-ride to Punta Róbalo had been just the opening act in what would be a long-lasting play that would see our two adventurers travelling from Panama's Caribbean coast *almost* to its Pacific coast – and on a route that would expose them to the varied and sometimes stunning geography of this Central American nation. It would also expose them to the limited dimensions of a Japanese micro-bus that would have been a bit of a problem for people with a Japanese build, but which for six-foot-two Brian was a lot of a problem.

Alex, its driver, had turned up with this machine after a wait of about fifteen minutes (probably from the other side of Panama) and had suggested that his two guests used as much of its interior as they could to avoid compression injuries or the onset of DVTs. Brian willingly complied with this suggestion, sitting himself sideways behind the front passenger seat where he could provide his legs with a modicum of room.

Sandra did likewise behind him, and the sardine can then moved off.

To start with, the drive took them along a deserted road cut through the marshy coastlands of Bocas Del Toro province, which had now been turned over to the raising of bananas and cows, two agricultural products that were rarely, thought Brian, ever seen together on a plate. It wasn't a particularly attractive area, not least because it was dotted with a number of domestic dwellings, none of which would earn a 'highly desirable' description in an estate agent's blurb. Without exception they were not just scruffy but they were also adorned with plastic beer crates, rusting oil drums, plastic sheeting and a dozen other varieties of junk. Maybe, thought Brian, he should restrict his travels to the pretty Cotswolds or maybe he should just close his eyes – until Alex had delivered his passengers to a more agreeable environment.

Well, eventually he did. After an hour or so and having joined the main road that would take them south, things began to look up – and go up. Yes, the lowlands, with their increasing evidence of human disturbance, were being left behind and in their place appeared the foothills of Panama's central spine of mountains: its very own 'continental divide'. Here there were no cows and no bananas, and very few habitations but just lots and lots of trees. Initially, these were both of the deciduous and evergreen variety, but as Alex dragged his microbus into the mountains proper, it was exclusively the evergreen that took over. It was all very scenic, and if it hadn't been for the degraded surface of the road and the omnipresence of deep potholes, it would have been a really enjoyable element of Brian and Sandra's journey – and Brian would not have been worrying about hitting his knees and his head all the time.

Anyway, there was a respite on its way. Alex determined it was lunchtime. Probably because they had just reached what seemed to be the only eating place on this route over the mountains, a tiny wooden-built hut that was perched above the road at the very apex of the mountain chain. Pre-lunch, it had all been up; post lunch, it would all be decidedly down. Just as soon, that is, as lunch had been consumed. This took very little time. Alex and his two charges were the tiny restaurant's only patrons, and whilst sandwiches, toasties and other delicacies were on offer, Brian and Sandra both opted for a can of ginger beer and a Twix. The prospect of at least two more hours in that Japanese nano-transport with an over-full stomach was just not very appealing. Neither, as it transpired, was the scenery on the southern side of the mountain chain as the land dropped down to the coast…

Its official guidebook description was 'a mix of scrub, savannah and crops'. But that description failed to convey the tired, scruffy, overworked nature of this part of Panama. It immediately made Brian think that he should seriously consider that pretty Cotswolds option, even though he'd been there many times before and even if its wildlife wasn't quite as exotic as that of Panama's. And then Alex finally reached the strip of squalor commonly known as the Pan-American Highway, and he began to weigh up the relative merits of Chipping Campden and Stow-on-the-Wold.

This stretch of the highway was just as bad as the stretch nearer Panama City encountered a few days before. And it also had the added 'bonus' of it running through the provincial capital of 'David' (a city named after King David of Bible fame – who might, thought Brian, lobby for a name change if he ever turned up here). It is a city of 150,000 souls, all of whom have to spend their lives in what at best looks like an extensive trading estate full of builders' yards and vehicle lots and what, at worst, looks like the result of a concerted effort to create the most hideous and ugly conurbation on Earth. But no. That was an exaggeration. Brian had seen far worse than David in his travels, but his reading of his Panama guidebook had told him that David was a relatively affluent city with an established middle class, and he would have 'expected better' – even though its residents had probably never even heard of the Cotswolds…

Brian definitely needed an uplift, and he soon got one, in more ways than one. This was because Alex had now turned off the Pan-American Highway, and was making his way back up into the mountains. It seemed that, because of the limited capabilities of his toy transport, he had been obliged to ignore a direct alpine route to their destination on the southern flanks of the central mountain chain, and instead go all the way south to the Highway and then travel north again – to reach Volcán. Yes, this was where he was now taking Brian and Sandra, a town that sits on an old lava flow from the (now quiescent) 'Volcán Barú', which at 3,475 metres is the highest point in the whole of Panama. Of course, this means that Volcán itself is a pretty elevated place, and indeed it sits at 1,400 metres above sea level.

So Brian and Sandra were now on their way through a rather more salubrious area of Panama in a very upwards direction, and Brian was getting a double whammy of uplift. Nevertheless, he was also getting a very numb bum. There was just so much time one could spend in a too-miniature-mobile, and he was desperate to see his growing ordeal at an end. So too, it appeared, was Sandra. She had recently become very quiet...

And then they were there. On Volcán's main drag, where Alex had parked his mini-machine. And after only a few minutes, a rather more robust 4x4 turned up, and this, it transpired, was to take Brian and Sandra on the last leg of their transfer to a place called the Mount Totumas Bellbird Lodge. Little did they know it, but only now would the really tough part of their trip get under way.

To start with, all was fine. Their new (uncommunicative) driver drove his big-boy machine along the road out of Volcán, further into the mountains, and it was very much a comfortable and distinctly un-cramped ride for his passengers. But after only ten minutes or so he turned off this tarmacked road onto a track that was rather more unrefined mineral than refined metalled and that might best be described as... indescribable. However, to give it a try, how about appalling, bone-shaking, atrocious, hugely distressing and apparently never-ending? On their previous travels, Brian and Sandra had made a habit of finding dreadful tracks up which to drive, but this one was a corker. And principally because it wasn't really a track at all, but more a dry river-bed littered all along its length with rocks of all sizes. The only relief on this hour-long ascent was where the 'track' was so steep and so uneven that two narrow strips of concrete had been laid to allow a vehicle to pass – just as long as its driver didn't take it off the strips... It was a hellish experience and one that only stopped being hellish when it came to an end. This it did when their vehicle pulled to a halt where the 'track' ended: just outside the alpine-looking Bellbird Lodge, the main accommodation building in the 'Mount Totumas Cloud Forest' eco-resort.

Its title was a bit of a giveaway. Because this particular eco-resort comprises 400 acres of remote cloud-forest wilderness bordering the huge cross-border La Amistad International Park. Oh, and at 1,900 metres (6,300 feet), it is easily the highest eco-resort in Panama, and arguably the one with the very best views! Yes, that tortuous, torturing climb had brought the lodge's newest guests to a place that lay just below the apex of that continental divide. Brian and Sandra would be spending the next two days at almost the summit of Panama's tree-covered mountain chain, and the views all around and especially those looking back to the Pacific coast were simply spellbinding. It was like being at the top of a really beautiful world – and a world stuffed with a whole new crop of beautiful birds.

However, that was for tomorrow. It was now late afternoon, and after being greeted by one of the resort's owners, a fit-looking guy by the name of Jeffrey, it was time for Brian and Sandra to settle into their generous room (one of just five in the lodge) and then to provide themselves with an aperitif before dinner. This was in the form of two bottles of IPA beer from a fridge – which reinforced Brian's original thoughts that the Bellbird Lodge had something of the youth hostel about it. It was all wood and all simple and it certainly didn't offer a conventional bar or much in the way of cocktails or spirits (and how would they even get the bottles up that track?). Brian knew, of course, that he was being his usual mean-minded self – and he also knew that he'd never in his life been in a youth hostel, so that made his mean-mindedness even worse. Perhaps he should settle on 'simple-alpine' instead, the sort of thing you might end up in on a budget skiing holiday. And if you were very lucky on that budget trip, you might also end up with the sort of food served at the Bellbird Lodge, which was as outstanding as all the food at the previous three lodges had been mediocre. Jeffrey's wife, it appeared, was the chef and she was the best chef yet to have been encountered in this country. The nosh was indisputably superb.

Unfortunately, the dining system involved the use of separate tables for the lodge's various guests. This meant that Brian and Sandra could not share their thoughts about the food with the other diners – and that Brian could not share his thoughts about anything under the sun with the other diners. He therefore resolved to share some particular thoughts with Sandra when they were back in their room. These, it soon became apparent, would concern the disappearance of the test card…

'Sandra,' he started, 'do you remember the test card?'

'You mean that thing on the telly with a picture of a girl in the middle?'

'Yeah. She was playing noughts and crosses with a stuffed clown. Slightly creepy really. But it did its job, didn't it?'

'Something to do with testing the quality of the transmissions, wasn't it?'

'Well, yes,' conceded Brian. 'But for most of us, it had a much bigger job, didn't it? I mean, it was what was shown while there were no programmes being transmitted. So in a way it worked like those two security guys who came into the pub with their two German shepherds…'

'You've lost me.'

'That really rough pub I worked in when I was a student – in the middle of Brum. I mean, when it was time to get everybody out, they'd turn up with their dogs, and everybody would get the message immediately – that it was time to clear off.'

'Still not with you.'

'Well, when the test card came on to the screen, it was just the same. You knew it was time to go, time to go to bed. And that was whether you intended to sleep there immediately or maybe after a few minutes of sexual exertions. But essentially the "day proper" had come to an end, and the next one wouldn't start until the morning. Whereas now… well, everything's twenty-four hours, isn't it? And there must be hundreds of TV channels pushing out all sorts of rubbish during the night, and with no test card to warn people of the error of their ways, more and more people not getting anything like the rest they need…'

'Oh come on, Brian.'

'No, it's true. And of course telly isn't the major threat to the nation's sleeping habits now. It's…'

'…smartphones.'

'Precisely!' confirmed Brian. 'Which is why as well as reintroducing a bit of downtime on telly at night – with just the test card on the screen – the same should be done for all mobiles. At 11.30, say, they'd all lose all their functions and if you switched them on all you'd see on your screen would be a little girl playing noughts and crosses with a clown. And I know most young people would happily watch a clip of a kitten accidentally activating a vibrator – for minutes on end – but even they might eventually tire of a non-moving picture that lacks either violence or sex. And then, who knows? They might turn off their machines and go to bed, and then be awake enough in the morning to learn something at school…'

'You'd better lobby for the test card to be there for about twenty-three hours a day…'

'Gotcha,' responded Brian. 'And maybe in the one hour of active time, they could broadcast repeated repeats of the Epilogue…'

That was it. Another solution to a pressing world problem had been successfully incubated, and it was now time for Brian to take his own advice and to get to sleep. But not before contemplating his extreme good fortune in having ended up at the Bellbird Lodge. It was, after all, situated in an area of Panama that could not just give the Cotswolds a run for its money but, when it came to out and out splendour, could beat it hands down. Yes, this Mount Totumas Cloud Forest place was both literally and metaphorically on a completely different level…

11.

$\mathcal{I}$t was the lodge's being on a completely different level that was responsible for the wind overnight. It was extreme. But up here at 1,900 metres, not in any way unexpected. Nor was the slight chilliness overnight or the noticeable freshness in the morning. Brian and Sandra were still in tropical Panama, but the climate at Mount Totumas was very different from that which they'd experienced at the three previous lodges. It was more temperate than tropical and it meant that when they set out for their morning walk, they were both wearing fleeces. It promised to get a little warmer as the morning wore on, but certainly not warm enough for tee-shirts and shorts. And anyway, there were apparently jiggers around, and as well as spraying themselves against the attention of these little buggers, both Sandra and Brian were keen to expose as little of their flesh as they could possibly manage. After all, playing host to a 'chigoe flea', was not high on their bucket list – especially if it was a female jigger, which apparently burrows head first into your skin, and in a way that allows it to breathe, defecate, mate and expel eggs while it feeds from your blood vessels! Oh, and then, when it has released its several hundred eggs, its body rots under your skin and this causes the sort of skin infections that end up as colour plates within the pages of medical tomes. It's all very unpleasant.

However, as soon as the walk was underway, thoughts of jigger attacks soon subsided, and Brian and Sandra focused instead on their companions for the morning. These comprised Jeffrey as their guide, a middle-aged American called Edward and his American/Panamanian daughter, Alexandra. Clearly, thought Brian, Edward had taken the need for good American/Panamanian relationships very seriously indeed – as would probably be confirmed by his Panamanian wife who was still back at the lodge. She had apparently been told that this morning's walk along the 'Big Tree Trail' was not only steep in sections but also over four kilometres in length. In fact, Brian had even considered keeping her company…

Anyway, his chance to play the wimp had passed, and having sorted out his walking companions, he now got on with the job of actually enjoying the walk. This was not difficult. After making their way through a band of secondary growth – which had resulted from allowing vegetation to return to what had once been an area cleared for worthless cultivation – the walkers were soon into a proper cloud forest with proper cloud forest trees, some of which were very large trees indeed. It was a joy for them all but, inevitably, a little bit of a problem when some serious bird-spotting got underway.

It cannot be denied that trees are essential for the forest birds – obviously – but these same trees also obscure these birds – obviously. It is one of the challenges (or trials) of observing birds in a wooded environment, and as often as not a challenge that can be met. However, when the trees are very, very tall, and the generally very, very small birds that live in them choose the tops of the trees to go about their business, the challenge can sometimes be too much. Finding the little blighters in one's binoculars is the first problem, but the second even worse problem is dealing with the strain that is then put on one's body. This is the strain that comes from peering through binoculars at something directly above one's head (as is so often the case). And it can easily manifest itself as a sore back and an even sorer neck – or possibly as a sore bum if, in one's eagerness to follow that tiny spot-crowned woodcreeper as it moves overhead, one has fallen backwards onto the forest trail. Normally, it has to be said, most people stay upright – just as, normally, most people acquire a stiff, painful neck.

Nevertheless, the effort and the discomfort were all worth it. Jeffrey managed to find for his group a really good number of different birds – such as a yellowish flycatcher, a slate-throated redstart, a mountain elaenia and, most exciting of all, a three-wattled bellbird, in full (only slightly neck-breaking) view.

Now, it may be recalled that the principal accommodation in the Mount Totumas Cloud Forest resort is the Bellbird Lodge, and this strange three-wattled bellbird is the reason that this name was chosen. It is also the principal reason for so many people fighting their way up that dreadful track to get here. This bellbird is a very special bird indeed, and special in more ways than one.

To start with, it is very shy, and it is more often heard than seen – but when it is heard (and it is always the male bird that is heard) it is unmistakeable. It sounds... well, like a bell. However, not any old bell, but an exquisitely tuned bell and a very loud bell. In fact, it is thought that the male bellbird's call is one of the loudest birdcalls on Earth, audible to humans almost a kilometre away. Which, for a bird that is around just ten inches long, is quite an achievement. So is the bellbird's learning its call, as it has been found that rather than having its call determined by instinct, a bellbird has to learn how to do it – from listening to other bellbirds. And the bellbird is obviously a good learner. Then there are those wattles – on (of course) the male bellbird.

Yes, it should be said at this stage that as well as leaving the bell-ringing to the males, the female bellbirds also leave the wattles to the males. The females have just olive plumage and yellowish streaked underparts – and not even a single wattle. This is in sharp contrast to the male birds, which have a white head and throat and otherwise chestnut brown plumage, but also three very prominent wattles. These long, slender, almost wormlike appendages dangle from the base of the male's beak and are for use in displaying to the lady bellbirds. This is where it gets very interesting and, for Brian, very thought-provoking. Because apparently these wattles can be as long as four inches when extended during songs and 'interactions' – but they remain flaccid even when extended. The bellbird shakes his wattles, but otherwise they hang straight down and are neither erectile nor under his muscular control.

Well, Brian was quite envious – on behalf of his fellow human males. What, he thought, would many of them give to have anything that could hang down that far in proportion to the rest of their body and that could legitimately remain flaccid? And then all they'd have to do would be to learn how to shake it, and of course sing like a sonorous bell. Brian reckoned it would be a doddle, and far less fraught in the 'interactions' department than it is under the current arrangements. Although, there again, arguably not quite as satisfying. And maybe not even as satisfying as the Turkish figs…

The five walkers had now been walking for nearly two hours, and much of that walking had been downhill but not quite as much as had been uphill, which is why, as reported by Jeffrey, they were now at an elevation of over 2,000 metres. As a reward for their efforts he suggested they stop for a rest below a huge avocado tree, and that they sample some of his prize-winning figs from Turkey. He had been carrying them in his rucksack, and it was now time to hand them out as a surprise but very welcome mid-walk snack. Brian had several, and as he ate them, he wondered how they had found their way from Turkey to the continental divide of Panama. He also wondered whether any of the local frugivorous bellbirds had ever sampled one. And then he wondered whether the second leg of the walk would be as demanding as the first. He wasn't unfit, but at 2,000 metres, everything was just that much more difficult, even when you're full of figs.

He need not have worried. There was a distinct downwards aspect to the rest of the walk, and there were still frequent stops to locate further bellbirds. Whenever one was heard, Jeffrey would lead the search for its whereabouts – but without success. Further bellbird sightings proved as elusive as common sense, and Brian and the rest of the party eventually made it back to the lodge with just that one good view of this remarkable bird under their collective belt. But that, along with the other birds they had seen and the forest itself, had been more than enough. It had been a quite wonderful morning – and, as it transpired, a little more wonderful than most of the afternoon would be.

Brian and Sandra did spend a good deal of time after lunch observing the action around the lodge's bird-feeder – which produced a whole string of new hummingbirds – but they did then observe the inside of their eyelids for some time thereafter. Maybe that up and down walk in the thin atmosphere of the cloud forest had been more demanding than they'd thought. And, anyway, they did want to be fully recovered for their dinner…

This proved to be a good 'un, and not just because the food was again excellent. No, it was mostly down to the company at Brian and Sandra's table: a couple from Utah by the name of Jim and Carolyn who had earlier suggested that there should be some shared Anglo/American dining. They, like Brian and Sandra, didn't particularly want to dine on their own. They were younger than their English table companions, and therefore, in Brian's mind, well capable of withstanding at least one of his sermons, and this evening it would be his practised monologue (and it was largely a monologue) on the subject of mankind's very limited imagination.

He started by talking about something apparently unrelated, and this was the current rate of immigration into Britain. He didn't dive into the politics of immigration but instead he introduced his audience to an analogy, and this analogy was to compare the circumstances of his home country to that of an already full bath of water. What he said was that over the centuries there had always been some immigration into Britain, but that it had been minimal. It had been at the rate of a slowly dripping tap. If anybody even noticed it, it was because it helped in a little way to keep the bathwater warm and it didn't measurably raise its level. Sometimes the tap even dribbled rather than just dripped. This was when there were sporadic peaks in immigration – such as the influx of Huguenots in the eighteenth century. But again, all they did was 'warm the water' some more by bringing in with them their much-needed skills. So, there had been nothing intrinsically wrong with immigration, and over many hundreds of years it had barely been an issue in Britain, and all it had done was enrich the lives of the indigenous population.

But now. Well, quite simply, he explained, the tap has been turned on full and nobody has any idea of how to turn it off. Gone are the drips and the dribbles, and in their place, there is a constant stream of new arrivals – and the bath is already beginning to overflow. One only has to take a car journey on any road in Britain, or observe how one's local towns and villages are gobbling up more and more once green land to realise that the crowded island off the coast of Europe is becoming ever more crowded by the day. And this is not, he stressed, any sort of comment on who is arriving from that always open faucet, but merely a recognition of the unprecedented volume of the flow. Never before, in the history of Britain, has there been such an enormous deluge of visitors to this country who have no intention of returning home.

Well, at this stage there was a palpable degree of restlessness in Brian's audience, so he quickly steered his lecture away from the present to the future. What, he asked, would Britain look like in fifty years' time, or indeed in one hundred years' time – if that tap was still running? And, in all likelihood, it would still be running, simply because the pressure behind it would only ever increase as the whole of the world ran out of resources and space, and more and more people sought out anywhere that offered more than just a miserable existence. But here was the point, he said. Wouldn't Britain be in just as miserable a state as everywhere else by then, with its population doubled or tripled, say, from its present level, and its ability to sustain such a huge number of people well beyond its capacity? Indeed, things might be far worse than this. After all, so much water will by then have overflowed the bath, that it's not beyond the realms of possibility that the floorboards beneath the bath will have rotted and the whole thing will have plunged down to the floor below in an explosion of ceramic pieces. Which is not to suggest, he explained, that the island of Britain would sink beneath the waves, but that it might well sink into unimaginable chaos – even before a similar chaos had overtaken the rest of the world.

He could see it. The attention of his audience was definitely slipping. So he quickly moved on to his concluding point – which was that human imagination seems to have a depressingly short range. It can cope with three or maybe even five years into the future – as is reflected in any sort of government planning – and sometimes it can even have a stab at something twenty or thirty years away, if it's something suitably nebulous or suitably unconnected with the present. But that's exceptional. For most of the time, humanity's imagination cannot cope with the long range. If fifty years is really pushing it (for anything), then one hundred years is simply inconceivable, and a thousand years – for our imagination – is… well, simply beyond us. And that is why nobody even attempts to contemplate the longer-term impact of effectively unrestrained immigration into Britain. Or how about the longer-term impact of the unprecedented increase in the global population as a whole and its associated impact on the rapidly disappearing natural world? For a species that claims to be the most intelligent in the world, Brian concluded, it seems that in flexing its intellect it has somehow managed to inflict its imagination with myopia. It's as though, he suggested, we are now almost blind, and we simply cannot see what we will soon encounter as a result of our arrogance, our stupidity and our woeful lack of imagination. We will stumble sightless to our doom…

Well, Jim and Carolyn were kind enough to say that they would remember this dinner for some time, but they didn't appear to want to join Brian's cult. Instead they seemed to want to focus on Brian's use of the bath analogy in his argument and how this might play out in a generation accustomed to just showers. Brian's response to this reaction to his presentation was to resort to an interlude of humour – of sorts – starting with his asking his American companions whether they were aware that there was a Scottish parrot called a macaw. Indeed, he assured them, this hardy bird of the macaw clan even had its own tartan. That was shortly before Sandra drew this interlude to a close by reminding Brian that the English were known for their manners and not for their gross imposition of their own brand of humour on unwitting friends.

And so it was back-in-the-bedroom time, and a chance for Brian to make amends to his wife for any discomfort he may have caused her – by embarking on his next 'what has disappeared from our lives'. And this evening the disappeared in question would be Popeye.

'Do you remember,' he began, 'that every Monday at five o'clock, a staple of kiddies' telly was *The Boatswain* and three Popeye cartoons?'

'I do,' responded Sandra almost enthusiastically.

'But do you remember that he had four lookalike nephews called Peepeye, Pupeye, Pipeye and Poopeye?'

'No. All I remember is his spinach and Olive Oyl and Bluto. And couldn't he do all sorts of things with his pipe? I mean, couldn't he even eat his spinach through the thing?'

'Yes. Quite right. Just another reason we never see his cartoons today.'

'What?'

'Well, think about it. A stereotypical oaf who settles all his problems with his fists. A guy with no empathy with the female lead, but just a belief that she was in some way his property. An inveterate smoker. A guy with appalling eating habits – stuffing those whole tins of spinach down his throat in one go. And then somebody with no recognition of racial or cultural diversity. No recognition of the impact of his behaviour on vulnerable viewers. And no acceptance that his role could possibly be taken over by a woman or by a member of the ethnic minorities. I mean, he hasn't got anything going for him, has he? No wonder he's been consigned to the scrapheap of culture.'

'Brian,' observed Sandra, 'I think it might be time you gave it a rest – and yourself a rest. We have another wonderful day to look forward to tomorrow, and it might be better if you embarked on it minus any thoughts concerning outmoded cartoon characters – or baths running over… You know, sometimes I think you just go out of your way to punish yourself. And anybody else in earshot, come to that…'

Brian got the message. It was time to bring down the shutters – and time to give some more thought to having three flaccid wattles. For many people, he concluded, it would be a great deal better than having only one…

12.

Brian and Sandra's room had an expansive balcony. Standing on it in the early morning – while Sandra was priming herself for action in the bathroom – was, for Brian, an almost magical experience. The early morning light, conspiring with the alpine views all around, was creating for him a truly memorable experience, one that might even join that premier league of 'the first observation of an oryx', 'the first experience of calvados', 'the first encounter with onanism' and 'the second encounter with coupling'. It really was that good, and it immediately made Brian eager to see more of this fabulous environment. Fortunately, he'd not have to wait very long. Because immediately after an early breakfast there was another walk to undertake. And this was a walk around what was called the 'Bajareque Trail'. It would be undertaken with Jim and Carolyn, a young guide called Ronaldo and two of the lodge's dogs who, over the course of the two kilometre trail, would end up walking and trotting something like ten kilometres. Indeed, Brian would become envious of their unlimited energy – but not, of course, of their unlimited intolerance to chocolate…

It started very auspiciously. Within only twenty metres of the lodge, and well before the trail had been reached, Ronaldo heard and then tracked down a spotted wood quail. These ground-dwelling birds are about as shy as a naked nun at a nudist camp, and they are extremely difficult to see. Unless, of course, you have a really good guide, who on this occasion was called Ronaldo and who appeared to be attuned to every single sound around him, and then more than capable of tracking down the source of that sound. How, thought Brian (not for the first time), do these chaps bloody well do it?

Well, he doubted he would ever know. Just as he doubted that he would ever see another resplendent quetzal in his life (he and Sandra had seen just one before – in Costa Rica – and they had both formed the opinion that this would be the only one they would ever see). However, they had not taken into account the likelihood of being led through a cloud forest by someone like Ronaldo. Which is why, only minutes after entering an area of secondary growth forest not far from the lodge, resplendent quetzal number two was located and then observed.

Despite being... resplendent, these birds are not that easy to find. In the first place they are not in any way noisy. Indeed, one Mayan legend concerning this bird (of which there are many) claims that the quetzal used to sing beautifully before the Spanish arrived, but that it has been silent ever since and will only ever sing again once their land is entirely free. So, finding one is all about seeing one and, given their appearance, one would think that this should not be that hard. After all, a resplendent quetzal is a big bird, with a body up to sixteen inches long – with another twenty-six inches of tail streamer if it's the male. It also comes with an iridescent green body and a vivid red breast – which might have something to do with its name. But, nevertheless, it seems more than able to blend into the canopy of the forest, and even when spotted by a proficient guide, it can remain essentially invisible to his amateur charges. And on this occasion, it did indeed take a lot of pointing and a lot of describing where it was before all of Ronaldo's quartet were able to spot it and properly observe it. When they did, they were all suitably thrilled.

And why wouldn't they be? A resplendent quetzal is an ace bird. In ancient Mesoamerican societies it was considered divine, and it was always associated with the 'snake god', Quetzalcoatl. Its iridescent green tail feathers were venerated by both the Aztecs and the Mayans, who regarded the quetzal as the 'god of the air' and as a symbol of goodness and light. So, in short, a bit like the antithesis of President Putin – not that the Aztecs and Mayans ever had the misfortune to meet him. They just had to cope with softies such as Alvarado and Cortés – the ancestors of that current crop of liberals in Spain…

However, returning to the current walk, it can be said with a great degree of certainty that the resplendent quetzal was a highlight – but, of course, not the only bird that Ronaldo found. There were quite a few others including a Swainson's thrush – not to be confused with a Swainson's warbler, a Swainson's hawk, a Swainson's flycatcher, a Swainson's antcatcher, a Swainson's fire-eye, a Swainson's sparrow, a Swainson's toucan or a Swainson's francolin. Yes, a certain William John Swainson, one of the early Victorian scientists who got around quite a bit, did leave his mark on avian nomenclature in no uncertain terms – and this was not surprising when one considers his dog-like energy levels. Because here was a man who returned from a 'scientific' trip to Brazil in 1818 with no less than 20,000 insects, 1,200 species of plants, drawings of 120 species of fish and 760 bird skins (!) – which still left him with enough puff to become a prolific illustrator of natural history and to have six children from two wives. No doubt, if he were here with Ronaldo's current party, he would be straining at the leash to get to the next stage of its walk, which was one that would reveal a whole new host of natural wonders – and specifically some of those within the realms of Panama's natural flora.

Brian and co had now climbed up through the forest to a patch of alpine meadow that was bordered by trees, all of which were exposed to a microclimate resulting from their proximity to a gap in the continental divide. And this microclimate was formed by the 'Bajareque mists', mists which streamed through this gap and draped the upland vegetation here to create what was not so much a cloud forest but more a rare and intriguing 'mist forest'. One only had to look at any of the branches of any of the trees here to see what this meant, in that they were covered in a profusion of epiphytes, many of which were remarkable bromeliads and ferns, surrounded by mosses and lichen, and some of which were absolutely astonishing orchids. Indeed, if one was a dedicated 'orchidophile' one would be overtaken by a shuddering orchidorgasmic experience at this point, such was the variety and beauty of the orchids on display. And if, as a dedicated orchidophile, one wanted to risk back injury, one would crouch down, bend over and use one's binoculars the wrong way round (which creates a field microscope) to observe some of the ground-growing micro-micro-orchids that Ronaldo was able to find. These are miniature treasures that defy description but delight the mind – and that should be treated as the treasures they are. Even if they are almost invisible to the naked eye.

It was a climax that couldn't be bettered, which is probably why Ronaldo decided to take his charges slowly back to the lodge along a route which eventually brought them to the 'vehicle track' to the lodge. Here it was only too easy to see why that 4x4 journey to this resort had been so demanding and why the journey back tomorrow would not be something to relish.

But that was tomorrow. There was still a lot of today to enjoy, and this enjoyment started with a stimulating lunch with Jim and Carolyn, where Carolyn showed Brian and Sandra her remarkable illustrated diary. It was a little work of art – albeit a very different sort of work of art to those observed mid-afternoon. This was near to one of the resort's satellite cabins, outside which there was a very popular rank of bird-feeders – and the little works of art on show here were more of those remarkable hummingbirds…

It was like a multi-coloured blizzard. A never-ending blast of flying jewels, each one of them seemingly defying the laws of aerodynamics – and Brian's ability to snap them with his new, rather upmarket camera (relatively speaking). This was just as well. Hummingbirds should be observed, not photographed. And particularly when they include such masterpieces as violet sabrewings, brown violetears, magenta-throated woodstars, purple-throated mountaingems and green-crowned brilliants. Indeed, with names such as these, it was easy to imagine the early ornithologists straining to find names that would do any sort of justice to these living pearls. They were, all of them, glorious beyond belief, and, of course, entirely incredible. Nothing in the natural world could combine such beauty with such agility and such speed, in an impossibly small body. Brian reckoned it was all done with mirrors.

He expressed this view when he was again seated with Jim and Carolyn – and Sandra – to enjoy another splendid Bellbird Lodge dinner. For some reason he wasn't taken entirely seriously. Not, that is, until he turned the conversation to the qualities of our current world leaders…

Yes, he'd switched from sorcery to supremacy, and in particular how in so many parts of the world, supremacy is in the hands of villains. It used to be, he explained, that these villains were largely found in a whole host of tin-pot countries throughout Africa, Asia and South America. But now, he suggested, villainy in its various forms had spread to most of the world's countries, even to those that could legitimately claim to be anything but tin-pot. So, he went on, there was now a gangster in charge of Russia, a despot in charge of China and a criminal idiot in charge of the USA. Add to this trio of nations countries such as Turkey, Venezuela, North Korea, the Philippines, Saudi Arabia, Sudan, Nigeria and Iran, and you could extend the list of villains to include bandits, murderers, thugs and serial thieves. And worse still, in many of these countries, the hoodlum/murderer-in-chief was accepted by its citizens as a legitimate leader – and even accepted by those who should know better as a legitimate attendee at something like a G20 meeting – rather than, as he should be, being carted off to jail for a brief spell before being taken out and shot.

Of course, it wasn't exactly perfect closer to home – as in Europe – where a bunch of chancers, carpetbaggers, delusionists and bullies had grabbed for themselves ultimate power and were busy bringing Europe to its knees. But at least they weren't overtly supressing their populations, overtly stealing from them – or ordering murders on the streets of provincial cities or on the premises of overseas embassies.

Well, Brian's audience didn't seem to know how to react to this indictment of so many of the world's leaders, and they certainly didn't know how to react to Brian's explanation of the cause of this outbreak of bandits and crooks. Because, according to Brian, it was all down to overpopulation, the relentless rise in human numbers that was starting to shape human behaviour. He went on to explain his theory by first drawing his table companions' attention to research into mice and rats that has demonstrated that when their populations were allowed to exceed 'comfortable density levels', all sorts of unpleasant things started to happen – like mayhem, murder and even cannibalism. Well, he proposed, the human race was now reaching plague proportions, and whilst there wasn't yet widespread murder or cannibalism there was definitely a good deal of mayhem about – and also the first signs of an evolutionary shift as a direct result of these changing conditions. That is to say that obnoxious behaviour – and especially cheating, the abuse of one's fellow man for one's own purposes and a dreadful indifference to the consequences of one's own actions – were emerging as the qualities one needed to survive in what will soon be a very brutal world.

So here was the first obvious sign of it: the rapid growth in the number of tyrant crooks in the world – and also a proliferation in the number of people who saw only positives in their egregious behaviour (known fittingly in the USA as Mr Trump's 'base'). Quite simply, Brian maintained, there was less and less room in the world for honest, moderate and thoughtful leaders, and less and less room for all those reasonable folk who wanted these sorts of leaders. They, he suggested, were destined to become the losers in this evolutionary race, and mankind, if it survived at all, would therefore become even more brutish and selfish than it already is.

At this stage of the proceedings, Sandra reminded her husband that there were limits to her tolerance of his apocalyptic opinions when expressed over dinner in the company of others – and that he had just exceeded those limits. However, Carolyn came to his assistance by supporting his analysis of the US situation and in particular how there was something deeply unwholesome about a bunch of people being prepared to accept what only recently would have been seen as completely unacceptable behaviour by their leader. Jim then also assisted Brian by asking his fellow diners whether they had ever considered that some people – like, for example, Calvin Klein – evoked subconsciously thoughts of words such as 'wine', 'shine', 'vine' and 'fine', but that others evoked words such as 'rump', 'lump', 'sump' and 'dump' – and indeed 'chump'? Yes, he concluded, their current president even had the right name for his nature – just like that guy in Russia who is named after a low-cost excrement container.

Well, Brian was impressed and delighted with his two new friends, and lost no time in informing his wife of this when they were back in their room. And he then lost no time in informing her of the subject of his next lecture on what had vanished from their lives. It was the Allen Scythe…

Fortunately, he didn't have to explain what he was talking about. Because, back home, next to the wood store, Brian had quite some time ago parked his own Allen Scythe – where it would now lie 'til the end of days. Years before, he had made the mistake of buying this second-hand monster and then trying to use it, and had quickly decided that he was simply not up to that task. This was because an Allen Scythe is a monstrous beast that was built between 1935 and 1973 (when men were men) designed to do the same job as a traditional scythe but with the power output of a substantial engine. This was used to drive the large solid wheels of the machine – and a very wide toothed blade at its front that slid back and forth horizontally across a set of stationary teeth to produce a terrifying scissor action. Of course,

Sandra already knew this, so his discourse kicked off with a reminder of just how unwieldy and dangerous these machines were, particularly in the hands of a mere standard-sized human...

'Yes,' he intoned, 'it wasn't just that these Allen Scythes were unwieldy. I mean, can you remember me trying to control it? It was like trying to steer a Sherman tank by using a couple of broom-handles attached to its rear – and it really did seem to be just that much heavier and more powerful than me. I suppose because it was. But then there was its clutch system. It only ever disengaged the drive to the wheels, and the bloody teeth at the front just went on chomping until you turned the damn thing off. It was indeed a wonderful combination of the unbelievably unmanageable and the incredible scary – and it could only ever have been made in Britain...'

'Very interesting, Brian, but...'

'However, that British aspect is all important,' interrupted Brian. 'It's what might mean that we should maybe think of bringing the Allen Scythe back!'

'Eh?'

'Well, think about it. A generation – or maybe two generations – of weedy, feeble little darlings who can't even cope with a suitcase these days unless it's got wheels on it, and who certainly can't cope with the rigours of modern life. Because, I suggest to you, they haven't had to cope with something like an Allen Scythe...'

'What? You're not proposing...'

'Yeah. Put it on the school curriculum. One hour's cutting the outfield each week with one of those bloody

118

Tin-Can-opy Tower

Canopy Lodge canopy stairway (?)

Tranquil Tranquilo Lodge

The best Deadly Sin

Big trees on the *Big Tree Trail*

Small bird on the *small twig*

The *MV Discovery* at sea

Not the *MV Discovery* on a river

Some impressive Emberá loincloths

Some expressive Emberá youngsters

A little boat and a big ship

A big ship and a big ship

A tight fit

Not a bridge

Chilling out on the Chagres

An El Otro Lado jaguar (?)

monsters, and they could soon cope with just about anything. They might even want to tackle changing a wheel on a car. Or having a conversation with an adult…'

'If they haven't cut their feet off first…'

'Yes. But that would be all part of its benefit: confronting the perils of antiquated British engineering. It would be so confidence-building, it would make men of them within weeks…'

'And women?'

'Oh, come on. Let's not go there…'

'And what about the fact that you couldn't manage it. I mean, it didn't make a man out of you.'

'Correction. I did manage it for quite some time. Sort of. And anyway, I was already a man. Brush-cutter and chainsaw accredited and all the rest.'

'Ah yes. That reminds me. Rest. If only…'

Brian took the hint. In fact, he had to. And he was soon lying in his bed occupied with no further thoughts about Allen Scythes, but instead with further thoughts about current world leaders. Why, he wondered, were they all quite so revoltingly ugly…?

13.

ow does one address a hiatus in Panama? That question had arisen in respect of this next day of Brian and Sandra's adventure, because whilst they were due to leave the Bellbird Lodge in the early morning, they were not due to catch a flight back to Panama City until late afternoon. This flight was from David's airport, and this was no more than two hours away from the Mount Totumas resort. There was therefore a six-hour gap that needed to be filled – and preferably not in the 'Enrique Malek International Airport', which was David's mysteriously entitled former US airbase, now turned into a civilian and frankly not very international facility (with flights from here going to just each of Panama City's own two 'international' airports). Well, the answer was 'take in a coffee *finca*'. Or more precisely, have a private visit to an established coffee estate just outside Volcán, where apparently there would be some bird-watching opportunities as well as a no doubt obligatory inspection of the estate's commercial activities. It wasn't a bad idea, but it wasn't an idea that filled Brian and Sandra with a great deal of enthusiasm either. Given the choice, they would have preferred to get back to Panama City on an earlier flight and thereby avoid having to deal with an intermission in their tour. It was, after all, just 'filling a gap'.

Anyway, to start with there was some purgatory to deal with, and after saying their goodbyes to Carolyn and Jim, Brian and Sandra were soon being agitated down the track. It hadn't got any better or any shorter since they'd been agitated up it. Needless to say, they were very relieved when they were back on a surfaced road, and even more relieved when they were collected by an extremely affable guy in Volcán, who would be their guide for the rest of the day. His name was Raoul, and he spoke very good English – and he had a comfortable car. This he used to transfer his passengers to the coffee *finca* just a few miles out of town, where they would be met by the son of the *finca*'s owner – and a remarkable manifestation of the amazing villainy of one Mr Manuel Noriega…

Miguel was the son, and he was waiting for his new guests in his venerable Toyota Land Cruiser, which was parked on the edge of a full-sized, fully usable, beautifully tarmacked runway.

Inevitably, this runway was the substance of Miguel's first story. And this story concerned how his family had, many years ago, created a little airstrip on this site, which had eventually caught the attention of Panama's frightful dictator, when he was at the height of his power. Indeed, so powerful was this terrible fellow, that when he 'asked' the *finca*'s owners to sell him the airstrip, they had to comply. If they had not, they might have lost a lot more than just their property. Anyway, in due course, the deal was done, and Noriega lost no time at all in converting what had been a simple grass airstrip into an operational runway that could accommodate aeroplanes up to the size of 737s – in order to facilitate the conduct of his drugs business. The criminal ruler of the country wanted a 'proper' private runway, from which he could send his drugs to the rest of Central America and then, of course, on to North America.

A project such as this, Miguel suggested, was as ambitious as it was blatant – but in the end it didn't work. Reality and the US caught up with the awful head honcho before this clandestine facility could be put into operation, and ultimately the airstrip-turned-runway reverted to the *finca*'s owners. All it is used for now is the occasional light plane of a visitor, the occasional sprint event organised by local car enthusiasts – and as a tangible illustration of just how bad people can be when they are allowed to have power. Oh, and how delusional they can be…

Well, having loaded his three guests into his Land Cruiser and having checked that no planes were about to land, Miguel drove his big beast across the runway and into the *finca* proper. Here he stopped after a few hundred yards to show Brian and Sandra the two varieties of coffee plants that were being grown on the *finca* (Arabica and Geisha) and to explain how both of these varieties were used. And this was when it occurred to Brian that he was really beginning to enjoy this 'gap filler' and that it might even turn into something of a highlight of the holiday.

He was reinforced in this view when they were then dropped off by Miguel at the start of a forest trail – and when Sandra reported that she too was changing her mind about this visit. It could be a very good visit indeed.

The forest trail was certainly very good. With Raoul's professional help, it revealed a whole pile of new birds, including quite a few woodpeckers, woodcreepers and wood rails, and an abundance of tanagers and tityras. It was a feast – right up until it was time to have a little less than a feast in the shape of a coffee (naturally) and some biccies. This snack was enjoyed on an elevated lookout in the middle of the forest, and was enhanced by a new spot. Yes, it was a Swainson's hawk (not to be confused with his thrush, warbler, flycatcher, antcatcher, fire-eye, sparrow, toucan or francolin – obviously…).

Anyway, soon after this snack there was a genuine (food) feast in store. Raoul had brought his charges out of the forest, and there on an open expanse of lawn was a table dressed for lunch – next to another table groaning with food – and Miguel and his charming wife whose name was Oxana. With a glass of wine in his hand – and having observed at close quarters the food that had been prepared for lunch – Brian was now firmly of the opinion that this coffee *finca* interlude would be a real highlight. And this was confirmed beyond any possible doubt after two further hours with Miguel, Oxana and Raoul. Brian and Sandra had fallen into a little offshoot of paradise, and they would be very sorry to leave it.

They did, soon after they had been recruited into the job of milling some sugar cane with the use of an eighty-year-old rosewood sugar press – and sobering themselves up a little with some of the resulting juice. But this was not before thanking their guests profusely for what had been a really memorable and really hospitable visit. Sometimes, thought Brian, pleasures can turn up when you are least expecting them. So too can odd sights…

It was back on the Pan-American Trashway, shortly after Raoul had joined it from the road from Volcán, and what it was was a collection of pilgrims. It was apparently Good Friday, and these Catholic pilgrims were making their way to some shrine near the Panama coast – on foot. And this meant that some of them who had come from Volcán had already been walking for a day and had another day to go. And then presumably they'd spend another two days walking back! Brian was at a loss to understand this, not least because Raoul had confided in his guests that the Catholic Church was all powerful in Panama – and it sometimes (or virtually always) abused this power, quite often in a blatantly pecuniary fashion. It hadn't built a runway, he said, but it could quite often behave itself in quite outrageous ways.

Anyway, another runway was eventually in sight. It was the Enrique Malek International Airport runway, visible through some wire fencing and half-hidden behind a row of fire engines. They brought a smile to Brian's face. Because here, at a recently rebuilt, shiny-looking airport, was an equally shiny-looking building housing two shiny-looking fire engines – with another seven fire engines lined up on a patch of grass to its side. The first of these seven was presumably the most recently retired engine, the second was the engine retired before that – and so on down to number seven, which looked as though it might have seen service with the US Airforce shortly after the attack on Pearl Harbour. And these seven old motors, Brian was convinced, had not been retained here for sentimental reasons or to form the nucleus of some Panamanian fire-fighting museum, but simply because nobody had got around to moving them. Like the other thousands of dead vehicles seen on this trip over the last few days, they had been abandoned where they had died, and they would remain there indefinitely. They would rot where they'd dropped, unwanted and unnoticed. Even if, when alive, they had all been bright, polished fire engines with bright, polished chrome (and even if they might [theoretically] be worth something as scrap).

Well, Brian was happy to see that the interior of the terminal building was free of any discarded material and then he became happier still when Air Panama announced that its flight back to Panama City would be leaving early because everybody had checked in. And presumably the pilot wanted to get home to start his Easter celebrations. In fact, the only downside to all this good news was that when Brian and Sandra arrived back at Albrook International Airport, they were too early for their transfer to their hotel, and they had to wait for quite some time for the arrival of Panama's number one aficionado of the *Fast and the Furious* franchise. That could have been the only reason that he drove like he did through the streets of Panama City. Or there again, it might have been a necessary defensive style of driving that allowed him to avoid killing a pedestrian on a flyover and avoid running into the back of a police car doing just 5mph on another flyover. Furthermore, it probably helped him avoid the odd car that did not comply with the local habit of just gliding between lanes but instead lurched between them without any prior notice. Brian and Sandra were quite relieved to arrive at their hotel for the night – right up until they walked into its reception area and took in its 'unusual' ambience.

This was a large, supposedly quite posh hotel, which had been chosen for its quality and its facilities – or so it was believed. However, it had the air of a tenement building and its facilities were essentially non-existent.

It didn't help that it was full of very noisy locals clearly enjoying an Easter break and that its sound insulation qualities had not been near the top of the designer's 'to do' list – if on it anywhere at all. And it helped even less that it was Good Friday. Because this meant that when Brian and Sandra had steeled themselves to tackle the greasy-smelling conjoined TGIF (which served as the hotel's restaurant), they were told that they could not have the G&Ts they tried to order at the bar, because they and all other alcoholic beverages could not legally be purchased on this holiest of holy days! Raoul was right. The Catholic Church in Panama was really abusing its powers, and in ways Brian would never have imagined. And why, he asked his wife, hadn't TGIF renamed itself for this particular evening 'DNTGIF' – as in 'Do Not Thank God It's Friday!'?

Well, peanuts and beer from the room mini-bar hardly constituted a boozy dinner, but they and CNN got Brian and Sandra through the evening, and the news even lifted their mood when it was reported that a ban had been imposed on a couple of Australian cricketers as a result of their ball-tampering activities. That, though, was about the only highlight and it did little to assuage the impact of the noisy guests of the hotel – and its noisy plumbing. There was only one thing to do: draw the evening to a close with the next instalment of Brian's lecture series, and tonight the subject of his gripping revelation would be British universities. When he announced this, he received an immediate response from Sandra.

'Brian,' she said, 'as far as I know, British universities are still with us. They haven't disappeared.'

'They have,' responded Brian. 'Where there used to be real universities full of researchers and thinkers, who would occasionally deign to do a little bit of teaching, we now have a bunch of *unis*, institutions that have about as much to do with genuine academia as does a bowl of maraschino cherries…'

'Maraschino cherries?'

'I couldn't think of anything better. And the point stays the same. Universities were places of learning for a genuine elite – in terms of their intelligence and their imagination – but they have now become swamped in a sea of *unis*, self-serving institutions which exist to swindle the mediocre in the name of universal higher education. Oh, and they also enable the current crop of vice-chancellors and their various hangers-on to become obscenely rich.'

'So you think that *real* universities are a thing of the past?'

'Yes – and no. I mean, I do accept that our real universities still exist – although even these institutions have ballooned into something really rather scary. But you can't convince me that a *uni* that offers a degree course in "events management" or maybe "football science", "gender studies" or even "comics" – as some do – is ever going to have a genuine place in the firmament of esteemed scholarly institutions, otherwise known as real old-fashioned universities.'

'I see...'

'Yes, and what's more, you can't get away from the fact that while there were many other venerable places of learning that provided all sorts of vital further education to generations of youngsters, they were not universities and should never have been turned into so-called universities. It does a disservice to them, a disservice to the real universities – and an even worse disservice to the tens of thousands of students who will graduate with a meaningless degree and a very sizeable debt, quite needlessly. Most of them will end up in jobs that need no real university education and many of them will rightly feel that they have been misled and duped, all in the name of some stupid species ideology that presupposes that half the population can somehow qualify as an elite. I mean, it's nonsense. Just absolute nonsense.'

'Brian...'

'No. I mean, I've done the calculations...'

'Oh, God...'

'Yeah. I reckon that when I went to university in 1967, I was one of the maybe 7% of the population who went to university at that time. Whereas now, 50% go to our current crop of humungous institutions – more and more of them, incidentally, with nothing like the requisite qualifications from school. And if that's not completely ridiculous, then just consider how many now get firsts compared to what happened in the late sixties…'

'Do I have to?'

'Yes. Because I recall pretty well that when I graduated, the percentage of graduates coming away with firsts was about 7%. It's now 25%. So if you do the arithmetic – taking into account the percentages of people going to universities in the first place, it means that in 1970, just 0.5% of the population could manage a first-class degree, whereas now it's 12.5%. Put another way, one in two hundred could manage that feat fifty years ago. Now it's one in eight. And that means either our young people are now twenty-five times brighter than they were fifty years ago – or that real universities have been engulfed in a tide of reprehensible political duplicity. You know, the sort of duplicity that has replaced a pool of genuine academic institutions with any number of modern-day, give-a-degree-away-for-nothing *unis*, which are doing little more than enriching themselves at the expense of us all. It's an effing disgrace.'

Sandra looked as though she wasn't sure how to react – to what was a genuine tirade on the part of Brian. But she eventually found some words.

'Right. Well, what should we do about it, Brian? Should we cut back to 7%?'

'Oh no,' responded Brian vigorously. 'I think we should go the whole hog. I mean, why stop at 50% of the population as its elite? Why not make it 100%? Hell, think of all those big garden centres that could be turned into *unis*. And then there's holiday camps and shopping malls and nursing homes and a thousand and one other places that could be given a motto and a coat of arms – along with a university charter – and Bob's your uncle. The whole country will become an academic elite, and *University Challenge* will have to be on every day of the week.'

'Brian, I think that's being a little unrealistic.'

'Yeah, I'm sorry. It ignores the fact that it's all completely… academic. 'Cos we're all screwing up the world so damn fast, that we'll all have reached oblivion well before we've reached any consensus on how to bring some sanity and honesty into higher education. Global warming isn't going to worry too much that Acton Catering College somehow morphed into the Metropolitan University of Middlesex. And a combination of resource depletion, unstoppable pandemics and nuclear annihilation isn't going to concern itself with the addition of yet another unnecessary humanities department to yet another British "seat of learning".'

Sandra didn't comment on what she hoped was the conclusion to Brian's rant.

And it was the conclusion – of a rant that was no more than a little letting off of steam, a natural reaction on Brian's part to his being frustrated by the power of an intrusive world religion. Sandra knew all this, because she herself had been less than impressed by missing out on that G&T. The good news – and Brian would know this too – was that by lunchtime tomorrow they would both be out of the reach of silly, superstitious practices, because by then they would be on a super (secular) catamaran.

Lunchtime, she thought, just couldn't come soon enough. Whereas the cockerel could...

14.

*I*t started at 4.30. How could that be? This hotel was in Panama City. Cockerels along with all sorts of other poultry tended to live in rural areas, not in the middle of conurbations. But maybe, thought Brian, this particular cockerel was sponsored by the hotel. It was kept within crowing distance by this hostelry in order to distract its patrons from the noise of televisions in adjacent rooms, two of which had been switched on at about the same time as the cockerel had sounded off (they were in the rooms directly above and below his and Sandra's own room). But whatever the explanation of the cockerel's presence, he wasn't the sort of chap to shirk in his duty. He started at 4.30 and he was still going when Brian and Sandra left their room at 8.00 to get themselves some breakfast – and to experience some sights that would forever be seared into their minds…

There was not a proper restaurant in this hotel, but just that dreadful TGIF which had been visited briefly the previous evening. However, there was a breakfast room, and it was on the way to this room that Brian and Sandra first encountered those other guests of the hotel who would remain in their memory for all time.

They were all local Panamanians – and presumably relatively wealthy Panamanians, as they were staying in this 'desirable' accommodation – and they were all either very fat or extremely fat. Now, a certain overabundance of human flesh is not a rarity these days, and both Brian and Sandra were really quite relaxed about the sight of merely oversized frames. However, rarely if ever had they seen on display such absolutely super-sized chubbiness, and so many examples of it gathered together in one place. Nor, in the case of the female 'extremely large' people, so many who had chosen such an alarming set of clothes with which to cover their bodies.

'Shrink-wrapping' was the term that immediately popped into Brian's mind, but within seconds this term was rejected. No shrinking of any sort was going on here, and the term that should have suggested itself first – and now did – was 'vacuum packing', as in the use of a film to fit as tightly as possible around the contents of whatever was being packed. And on this occasion what was being packed were some huge bulbous bodies and the 'film' used in the packing process was uber-tight tee-shirts and shorts. Never, thought Brian, in the history of womankind has so much been covered by so little and to such dreadful effect.

Here were grossly obese women who, through some unimaginable process, had been squeezed into clothing that was now stretched over their hyper-pneumatic bodies in a way that revealed every single bulge, mound, crevice and crack. It was unspeakably awful and, more than this, exceptionally puzzling. Why, thought Brian, would anybody who owned such a frightful frame wish to exhibit it to the world in such a brazen fashion? The answer, of course, was that within this particular tranche of Panamanian society, it *was* the fashion. To parade one's wealth – and one's vigour and one's value – one first had to equip oneself with a barrage-balloon figure and then one had to flaunt this barrage-balloon physique in all its horrible detail, even if it meant that the odd naïve foreigner might be put off his muesli or indeed scarred for the rest of his life. Yes, this wasn't a display of unintentional or unwanted grossness, but instead the ultimate result of a concerted effort to become gross, a practice that was something akin to the Mauritanian custom of fattening up their underage virgins. God help them, he thought…

Of course, there were 'big' men as well, but their bodies weren't quite so intimately defined. It was just more a case of barrel bellies beneath distended shirts and, above these bellies, lots of enormous jowls. And frankly, men just aren't equipped with quite so many crannies and mounds. They also don't add to their alarming appearance by painting their faces and pulling their hair back across their heads. Nor, no matter how hard they try, can they develop a rear that has more in common with a pair of medicine balls than it does with anything one might use for sitting.

Brian could see from Sandra's almost-protruding eyes that she was having as much trouble as he was in processing the sights that surrounded them. But he could also see that he was being rather too judgemental, if not a little intolerant in his thoughts. If this is what they chose to do in Panama, then that was entirely their affair. But even so… it might be possible to ignore the display of gargantuan manhood, but it was simply impossible to ignore the display of the equally gargantuan womanhood, particularly when it was so flaunted and so ubiquitous – and in such close proximity, as it was in the breakfast room. It was like having one's first meal of the day in a surreal exposition of the sort of flesh one would normally associate with certain sea-going mammals. And there wasn't even any muesli. All that was on offer was a collection of unappetising calorie-full 'stuff' that was nevertheless being tipped down the throats of the local heavies with considerable relish. They were simply shovelling it in.

It was an eye-opener and at the same time an appetite depressor – even if there'd been anything available to stimulate an appetite. Brian and Sandra just had to make do with some coffee and toast, whilst reassuring each other that they weren't being unduly censorious but that they had simply become the victims of an extraordinary convention in this country. Which was the ostentatious display of inflated female frames that not only left nothing to the imagination but that also left one feeling that a lack of common sense was an integral part of the local culture. It appeared that it wasn't just the driving in the wrong lane of the Pan-American Highway or the weird operation of the national airline that hinted at this cultural curiosity, but also what passed for feminine beauty in this country – and feminine allure… Don't be discreet and reserved in your approach to men, but just expose yourself in all your gross anatomical detail, whilst at the same time making it very clear that you can steamroller their emotions with ease – along with anything else that might get in your way…

Anyway, Brian and Sandra left the breakfast 'canteen' feeling full not of food but of guilt. Had their middle-class, middle-weight-at-most attitudes led them to condemn a whole nation and its ideas of what constituted female beauty? Or, there again, had they reacted quite normally to what was no less than a childish practice that would inevitably lead its practitioners into a life of poor health and poor mobility (one young super-large woman with three children in tow was already reliant on two walking sticks to enable her to tackle a short flight of steps)? Only one thing was certain, Brian decided. He would continue to prefer women who kept their bodies trim and for most of the time well away from the practice of vacuum packing. Even in swimwear there should be just a little that was left to the imagination.

Indeed, it was always good, he thought, that the imagination was given a work out now and again, and no more so than when one has a couple of hours to kill and one has tired of the novel one is reading. This happened mid-morning for Brian – while Sandra was fine-tuning the packing – and he put his imagination to work by attempting to visualise the impact of fashion-obesity in the natural world and whether it could possibly be sustainable in any way. Could one have a successful portly parrot, for example? No. Could one have a really plump howler monkey – who would have to stick to the sturdier branches of trees? No. Or how about an oversized ocelot? No way. In fact, the more he attempted to visualize any creature in the natural world that had put on excessive weight – not in the interests of hibernation – the more he realised that it couldn't happen. It is only that apex animal called man, gifted with more intelligence than any other animal on the planet, that can survive (at least for a time) with a body that has been pumped up by excessive eating in the name of making itself attractive to the opposite sex. And people wonder why we are rapidly destroying our world…

Anyway, eventually it was time to report to reception to wait for the transfer to that eagerly anticipated catamaran. Here Brian and Sandra met a couple called Mona and Richard, who were two elderly Brits now living in Canada. They were waiting for the same transfer – and unfortunately they would wait indefinitely to become in any way interesting. As Brian and Sandra suspected immediately, and as would become only too obvious over the forthcoming week, Mona and Richard were irredeemably dull and equally irredeemably unresponsive. It was a terrible condemnation of two otherwise very nice people, but it was true. Although, there again, to their credit, they weren't at all fat.

They were also, very obviously, as pleased as Brian and Sandra were to see the arrival of a minibus outside the hotel, followed by the approach of a fairly diminutive Panamanian who introduced himself as José and who then invited them to follow him to the bus. All four reception dwellers did this, and as two of them boarded the vehicle they immediately recognised Linda and Wayne from Tranquilo Bay. There was an immediate outburst of mutual recognition and extravagant greetings, which only stopped when it was thought proper to acknowledge that there were two others on the bus as well: a pair of Americans who went by the name of Angela and William and who would become, with Linda and Wayne, some very serious chums for the next few days. None of this four could have been dull if they'd tried…

So… next up was a trip in the minibus out of purely urban Panama City and into its marina-land, a place that looked as incongruous in this Central American country as did a functioning neuron in Donald Trump's brain. But that was to ignore that this was Panama City and not the down-at-heal rest of Panama. So its ranks of stylish and even opulent-looking boats looked hardly out of place at all against what was now the distant and rather splendid-looking skyline of this money-pot town. Wealth, however it might be accumulated, breeds wealth, and sometimes this wealth comes in the form of luxury yachts – within which there might just be a really inviting, almost chic-looking catamaran…

There it was: the imposing *MV Discovery*, a double-hulled floating hostelry which would prove to be as different from Brian and Sandra's previous hostelry as it was possible to be. To start with, it looked beautiful from the outside. It was 110 feet of sleek naval architecture (built in Tasmania!) with, above its waistline and below its bridge deck, two glass-encased decks that promised even more style within.

Neither Brian nor Sandra was disappointed when they had boarded it. They were taken directly to its upper enclosed deck which comprised an expansive and elegant lounge-cum-dining-room, complete with floor to ceiling glass walls, an inviting well-stocked bar and, through a door, a really professional-looking kitchen. Here they were plied with drinks and some light lunchtime snacks – and were introduced to their fellow shipmates for their forthcoming voyage. As well as their minibus companions, there were four smiley Germans, a fit-looking American couple, a mismatched American couple (of which more later) and a single American lady (of which not very much more later). That made a passenger complement of just seventeen souls – on a boat which could accommodate twenty-four paying guests. And it looked as though that would make for a very pleasant trip. So too would the passenger accommodation. This was on the deck below: twelve small but beautifully appointed cabins, all equipped with picture windows and the sort of one-piece bathroom that one would find on an upmarket spacecraft – if such vessels should ever get built before we've managed to demolish the world. Brian and Sandra's was 'mid-ship', and before the *Discovery* had weighed anchor and set off, it provided them with a really fine view of the almost incredible outline of Panama City, a conurbation composed on its seaward side of a multitude of tall and presumably dubiously financed buildings, none of which would have been out of place in any other of the dubiously financed metropolises on the planet.

Further impressive views were available as, after the obligatory safety drill, the *Discovery* left the marina and made for the open sea. Brian and Sandra, together with fifteen other guests and eleven crew, were now on the first leg of a seven-day cruise that would see them exploring a little of Panama's Pacific coast before transiting the

Panama Canal to explore a little of its Caribbean coast. And it would prove to be as good if not better than they could ever have imagined.

Anyway, before that got underway in earnest, it was the *Discovery* captain's responsibility to find somewhere to head for today, and that somewhere was the *Islas de las Perlas,* otherwise known, not surprisingly, as the Pearl Islands. This extensive archipelago comprises 200 or more islands and islets and sits about thirty miles off the coast of Panama in the Gulf of Panama. It was once famous for the number of... pearls that were found in its waters. Indeed, it didn't take long for the conquering Spanish to discover this and even less time to wipe out the Indians who lived there. They even managed to massacre twenty or so tribal chiefs who were apparently torn to pieces by the conquistadors' dogs. Which, as well as being savage beyond belief, also meant that the Spanish then had to import another batch of lowlifes to harvest the pearls. And it is their descendants who now live on the islands and sometimes share them with contestants in such uplifting reality programmes as *Survivor* – and sometimes even with such characters as Bear Grylls in the making of his own uplifting series of programmes. And whilst this all sounds really quite distressing for the islanders, it is arguably a little better than their being ripped to pieces by vicious dogs. Particularly if they are not obliged to watch any of the resulting television output.

The *Discovery* anchored off one of the archipelago's islands at about 6.30, and soon after this there was a presentation in the lounge on the indigenous Emberá

Indians (found in Panama and Colombia). Then there was an associated presentation on the environment of Panama's Darién province, the impenetrable jungle area of the country that borders Colombia and that still provides a permanent interruption to that super-long Pan-American Highway. That famous road might stretch from Alaska to the tip of South America, but in Panama it encounters the 'Darién Gap' and here it stops. If one wants to continue south from North and Central America, one has to take a boat and continue one's driving in Colombia – which, as far as Brian was concerned, was a great slap in the face for modern civilisation, and a very promising outlook for tomorrow's planned schedule. Because tomorrow, all the *Discovery's* passengers were to be taken into this wildest of all gaps. But that would have to wait. Now the presentations were concluded, it was time for dinner, and time for Brian to make sure that he and Sandra ended up on the same table as Linda and Wayne and Angela and William. This wasn't too difficult, and very soon, Brian and Sandra had learnt what their Tranquilo Bay companions had been up to since Tranquilo Bay – and what Angela and William had been up to for much of their lives. For William, this had included his being a vice-president of a software company – which apparently had nothing to do with furnishings or cushions, but something to do with computers. Inevitably, all these four people also learnt something about Brian, which was that he just didn't know when to shut up and could sometimes be almost annoying. Like when he invited them to give him their views on what really irritated them about modern popular entertainment. (He'd thought, on this first evening together, he should keep matters pretty light-hearted, and not steer the debate into areas such as assisted dying or the nature of the impending apocalypse.) And he was right. Even Sandra willingly followed his lead, and offered up her pet irritation – which was one that dealt with the end-credits of programmes and films shown on TV.

Why was it, she asked, that after devoting a little piece of one's life to a carefully crafted production, one was then denied the ability to discover the names of those responsible for the production – or those who featured in the production – by the broadcaster's desperate insistence on telling us 'what was up next'? Because, as likely as not, this insistence would involve the shrinking of the credits to just a sliver of screen, while at the same time giving the details of the forthcoming offering the lion's share of the screen – and then talking over the end-credits music which may well have been crafted with the same degree of care as the principal production itself. Angela agreed with the egregious nature of this practice and suggested that the desperation for its use stemmed from the youthfulness and the immaturity of those responsible for most of broadcasting these days. They were little more than children, she maintained, and they believed everybody had their own childlike attention span and therefore needed to be captured before they had turned to another channel or picked up their iPhone. They might never, she said, ever grow up.

She then went on to offer her own pet irritation, which was the insistence of these same children to coat every modern TV production – and particularly promising documentaries – with so much superfluous and intrusive music that they were rendered unwatchable. She'd lost count, she said, of the number of times she'd started to watch a programme, only to abandon it after five minutes when the cascade of strings or the interminable plinky-plonk of piano music had made it entirely unbearable.

This is when Linda came in to observe that any documentary these days was a product of the 'how to make a documentary by numbers' school of production techniques. And she then went on to explain that what she meant was that it was now effectively illegal to produce a documentary that was not preceded by a lengthy introduction of what the documentary was to include and thereafter peppered with either meaningless recaps of what had gone before or irritating previews of what was to come. It was, she said, another manifestation of the Trump-like attention spans of the current crop of juvenile producers, who simply had no idea that a more mature audience not only didn't need this stuff but also found it insufferably tiresome. Was there nobody out there, she asked, who had an ounce of originality in his or her approach to documentaries?

No, there wasn't, insisted Wayne. But there were far too many juveniles who appeared to be devoting their lives to the creation of an unending stream of unwanted trailers. Indeed, he suggested, if the effort that was expended on redundant trailers was diverted into the programmes they trailed, the world would be a far better place and he wouldn't get quite so exasperated quite so bloody often.

This is when William added his voice to the conversation, and he used his voice to admit that what really irritated him above all else was the expectation that the mumbled words on so many films would be heard and understood by anyone who had invested time in watching them. What was the point of having a scriptwriter, he asked, if what he'd written was so badly enunciated by the actors that they might as well have been reciting a nursery rhyme in Welsh?

This complaint received universal approval, although Brian did wonder whether all the complaints so far had really dug into the depths of irritation – or indeed whether they had even scraped the surface of what might be considered somewhat controversial. So he thought it was time that he made his own contribution to the debate. This he did by asking a question, and the question was: 'If nobody would accept a commercial film about Martin Luther King where one of his family members was played by a white person, why is it any more acceptable to cast a play at the RSC in Stratford where King Lear has three daughters, two of whom are white and one of whom is not? What makes it OK to make a fool out of Shakespeare – and of those who go along to watch his work – but not OK to make a fool out of a saintly black activist (who was very definitely black)?' Nobody provided an answer to Brian's question, so he provided one himself. It was, he told his silent audience, because diversity now trumped (or presided over?) any bothersome things such as talent, merit and credibility. And that wasn't just irritating, it was really bloody annoying.

Well, so much for his attempts at light-heartedness. Sandra made it very plain that she wasn't at all happy with Brian's detour into such contentious territory, and insisted he used his mouth just for eating and drinking for the rest of the meal. He would have to wait until they were back in their room before he could use it to utter any more words.

That insistence didn't quite work, but Brian didn't get into full flow again until he was tucked up in bed – and even then the flow was short-lived. He'd embarked on another of his 'what has disappeared' lectures, and had done little more than introduce its title before Sandra drew it to a close. On hearing it would be about the almost total disappearance of body hair from the female form, she informed her husband in no uncertain terms that there was nothing about this that she didn't already know. And furthermore, unlike antimacassars, there was a good chance that it would make a comeback – at least in some areas – and therefore it didn't qualify as something that was lost forever, or indeed something that had passed, 'the disappearance of which we may hardly have noticed'.

Brian could find no response. Sandra was right, and he knew he had made a bad choice. In no way now was he going to be allowed to discuss East German athletes, different waxing techniques, stick-on eyebrows or decorative merkins. Instead he'd just have to get himself to sleep. But not before giving some final thoughts to enormous women and the enormous problems they would have in the restricted surroundings of the catamaran's bathrooms. Just how much give, he wondered, was there in all that... pulp? Probably, he suspected, not nearly enough.

15.

he *Discovery* had been on the move overnight. It had set off at 2.00 am to commence a four-hour trip that would take it away from the Pearl Islands and down the Pacific coast of Panama's Darién province. This meant that when Brian peered out of his cabin window at 6.30, he found himself looking at a little slice of this wild, largely uninhabited part of the country. The captain had anchored his craft on this sunny Easter Sunday in an idyllic spot just off the coast, and the first activity of the day was the exploration of this coast at close range. Directly after breakfast, the catamaran's two tenders were filled with a full complement of expectant adventurers, and with José in one boat and his colleague, Juan, in the other, they both set off for a 'ride around the bay'.

This was a very leisurely affair that allowed all aboard the two vessels to have a really good look at some of the local vegetation and at some of the local birdlife. This latter category included spotted sandpipers, little blue herons, a couple of whimbrels and a solitary osprey, none of whom, Brian noticed, seemed to be suffering from the heat in the way that he was. It was still relatively early in the morning, but it had already become ferociously hot, and Brian's thoughts increasingly turned towards the prospect of a nice cooling sluice in a shower. And, not for the first time, he wondered how people coped in these tropical climes – when they had rather more to do than just idle around and when they didn't have easy access to either some shade or a shower.

Anyway, after returning to the catamaran – and having had that sluice – Brian was wondering something else, and this was whether he had ever before associated pearls with submarines. This was because he and his fellow passengers were being treated to a pre-lunch presentation on pearl fishing. In particular it was being revealed how over-exploitation of the oyster beds off the Pearl Islands had denuded the easier-to-get-at oyster beds by the middle of the nineteenth century, and that this had prompted a German-born American inventor and engineer by the name of Julius Kroehl to set about building a submarine that would facilitate the overexploitation of the deeper oyster beds – and of course make him rich in the process. And he did produce his submarine, and with a great deal of effort he got it shipped (in parts) from New York to Panama and eventually as a complete vessel to the pearl hunting grounds of the Pearl Islands. However, he had made a literally fatal mistake. He had dreamt up his idea and built his forty-foot vessel in 1867, which was just four years before people began to understand the cause of decompression sickness or 'The Bends'. So, even though he and his fellow submariners did succeed in collecting pearl-bearing oysters from depths of 100 feet and more, they also succeeded in becoming very unwell and incapable of participating in further dives. This was good news for the deep-water oysters, but not such good news for Mr Kroehl and his investors – or for the submarine which was abandoned on one of the uninhabited islands in the Pearl Islands archipelago. And it is still there to this day, not yet rusted away completely, but unlikely ever to be put back into service. Even assuming there were still any oysters left to exploit...

Well, this was all very interesting, but stories of ancient submarines would not constitute the highlight of the day. That would not happen until after lunch had been consumed, and it started with the arrival of two scruffy-looking wooden boats, each fitted with a canvas canopy and two enormous outboard motors. These motors, it was explained, would enable these boats to make their way at (great) speed up a nearby river and so deliver the *Discovery's* passengers to a genuine Emberá Indian village within just fifty minutes. Brian and his companions were going to conduct a bit of amateur anthropology – and to start with, enjoy some Darién-style air-conditioning – courtesy of those enormous engines. The two boats didn't so much race up the river as shoot up it, and the resulting gale in the open boats provided a very welcome relief from the heat. Right up until the boats turned into a narrow, mud-banked creek up which they were obliged to glide at no more than walking pace. Without that cooling blast of air, Brian soon became very hot, but it didn't matter. He was so distracted by this magical waterway. The river had been bordered by an unbroken expanse of trees, but along this creek, the trees created an extraordinary natural tunnel, and their exposed sinuous roots gave an almost other-worldly feel to the boats' passage along it.

Ultimately, this last leg of the water-borne part of the journey came to an end – when the level of the water in the creek fell below the draft of the boats. They could go no further. But fortunately, they didn't need to. Because they were now at the village's 'landing stage': a wide plank of wood with a rope handrail, laid across a muddy shore and surrounded by lots of beautiful village children. And these children really were indisputably beautiful; the very young village boys dressed in bright red loincloths and the young village girls in multi-coloured skirts and with flowers in their hair. They looked as though they'd been dressed for some exotic Hollywood movie – but they were real. And, as soon became apparent, they were disarmingly hospitable.

This hospitality manifested itself not in words, as they seemed to have no English. Instead it took the form of their taking the hands of their new guests and then leading them away from the landing area towards a wide green boulevard cut through the forest and edged with what were quite clearly carefully planted decorative trees. Brian quickly came to two conclusions. The first was that the village he was heading towards must have been there for some time, and the second was that it would probably be well-ordered if not completely delightful. And indeed, it was both.

The walk had taken nearly twenty minutes – and for none of those minutes had he been abandoned by his two young escorts, two very young girls who had not been abashed to hold his hands all the way to the village.

Only then did they release him, and with Sandra, who had been released by two young male escorts, he took in his first view of the village he now knew was called 'La Chunga'. It was a fine place, a settlement made up of dozens of thatched wooden houses raised on stilts, all set within a huge cleared area of the forest with, at the centre of this clearing, a large open-sided village hall. Around this were lots of village ladies who were tending a number of artefact-covered stalls and quite a lot of village men who were clearly supervising proceedings, as in 'they were doing nothing'.

Brian immediately went into acute observation mode and observed quite a number of things. These included the fact that the villagers all looked well and some of them (especially the women) very well fed. There seemed to be no poverty here and, whilst they weren't sharing in the wealth of Panama City, they were probably a lot better off than many of the rural Panamanians Brian and Sandra had previously encountered – and they lived in rather more salubrious surroundings. They also wore a lot more tattoos than one's regular Panamanians, but a lot fewer clothes…

Yes, the men sported tattooed necks and torsos, but wore just the same red loincloths as the little boys (only theirs were rather longer, and in some instances outrageously longer, and in Brian's mind not quite credible). The women, too, were 'sparingly' dressed and wore skirts around their bottom halves and just bead necklaces around their top halves. Accordingly, there was an abundance of naked breasts in La Chunga, and it was impossible not to notice that some of these obvious orbs were not of the mature variety but of the awkward adolescent variety. Brian would have to be very circumspect in the use of his camera. Particularly if he wanted to take a picture of the chief. Brian had been told that this was entirely in order, but the chief was currently standing in the middle of the village hall and behind him were standing two village beauties – with four outstanding orbs…

Anyway, Brian was now happily distracted by the presentation being made by the chief's English-speaking *aide-de-camp*. He was telling his audience of visitors all about the establishment of the village and how it now operated, and a little about its culture. He also mentioned the skill of the village women in producing a wide range of jewellery, pottery and assorted woven goods. This was at the end of his presentation and it was the signal that it was now time for a bit of retail therapy. It was time for the visitors to visit those artefact-covered stalls and to part with some of their American dollars.

Brian and Sandra invested in some earrings – for Sandra (of cuff-links and studs there were none). And with their highly portable purchases they then participated in a group walk around the village, which revealed more tidiness, more children, a few dogs, a pied puffbird, a keel-billed toucan, and a satellite dish. It also confirmed that its residents enjoyed a rather simple but quite attractive way of life. Brian knew it was all too easy to be patronising about what he saw, but it was even easier to see that these folk didn't warrant any patronising at all. They were clearly quite content with their lot – or at least as content as anybody can be with his or her lot – and they were more than content with the prospect of a little bit of dancing…

The catamaran gang had now been brought back to the village hall and had been seated around its edge in order, it appeared, to witness some tripping-the-light-fantastic by a number of the village residents. Proceedings commenced with some of the more mature members of the ensemble doing their thing while being accompanied by some of the village musicians. And variations on this theme of (respectable) adult entertainment continued right up until the climactic performance. This was something called the 'parrot dance', and rather disconcertingly it was about to be performed by six young girls between the ages of about eight and thirteen, none of whom was wearing a parrot costume or even a liberty vest. They were, like all the other girls and women in the village, dressed in just skirts and necklaces of beads.

It was a sort of clash of cultures: one that sees nothing to be ashamed of in the human body – even if the body is that of a young pubescent girl – and one that is now shackled by the fear of potential abuse and therefore regards all displays of young flesh as a cardinal sin and something to be avoided at all costs.

Well, Brian soon realised that he was very much a product of that latter culture, and as much as he was an advocate of freedom of expression in all its forms, when the form it took was a naked budding chest, it was all a little disturbing to say the least. And he could hardly just close his eyes. That would be bloody rude. So instead, as the six nubile young maidens did their routine, he tried to concentrate on their feet and their faces, whilst at the same time contemplating what might be a realistic solution to the threat of erosion on the east coast of England.

These tactics worked quite well, and he only abandoned them when he realised he could legitimately devote a minute or so to re-tying his shoe laces. By doing that, he wouldn't need to look at the dancers at all. However, as much as he thought this new move a brilliant idea, it was not. It was a terrible mistake – primarily because it didn't allow him to see that the dancers had interrupted their routine to initiate some audience participation, and he only realised this when just in front of his now neatly tied shoes appeared a pair of diminutive bare feet. As he then looked up, he discovered that they belonged to the eldest of the parrot troupe, that is to say the one with the most obvious breasts…

Given even a few seconds more, he might have thought of a suitable excuse – an old war wound or some imminent incontinence for example – but he had no time at all, and when his prospective dance partner extended her hand, he took it and then he took to the floor. He was about to spend the next few minutes of his life with a half-naked pubescent girl in full view of the girl's family and friends, his own companions from the catamaran – and his wife. God help him, he thought, if somebody was filming all this and happened to have a penchant for posting stuff on YouTube.

Matters were not helped by the fact that only two other visitors had been recruited into the dance. They were both women, which simply meant that Brian was now outnumbered by eight to one on the dance floor and that he was quite clearly an unwilling centre of attention and a cause for huge amusement. Those of his companions who were still seated were not only treated to an exhibition of his maladroit dance moves but also to his 'I'd really rather be anywhere else' level of embarrassment. At least, he thought, the parrot dance didn't call for any close clinches, and with the disparity in height between his own six-foot-two frame and his partner's much-less-than-five-foot body, their eyes were unlikely ever to meet, and his eyes were even more unlikely to have a close encounter with either of her outstanding features. That said, it was still a little taste of purgatory, and his relief when it ended was immense. Albeit short-lived.

It was as he was recovering from his ordeal and as José was gathering up his charges for the return to their boats. Their visit to the village was now coming to an end and it was time to leave, time for them to make their way along that lovely tree-lined boulevard – and back to Western acceptable norms. Again, he was taken by surprise, and by that very same girl. Yes, she had approached him from behind, and before he could do anything about it, she was holding his right hand tightly and had clearly appointed herself as his escort for the twenty-minute walk back to the boats.

This entrapment of a senior by a minor was a cause of renewed amusement – particularly for Sandra. And the amusement was sustained as Brian was marched out of the village and almost straightaway found himself estranged from the 'pack'. His escort was not interested in birds or other diversions on the way to the boats, but the members of the catamaran pack were. So, as they stopped to make their observations (of such things as a black-chested jay!) Brian and his pal simply went striding on. There was no way he could communicate with her and no way of telling her that if he ran into an off-duty sergeant from the Met, he would probably have his name taken in order for it to be placed on the sex-offenders' register back in Britain. And then it got even worse. Brian had remembered something, something that had been imparted in that introductory presentation about the culture of this village, namely that marriages here were somewhat informal affairs!

Christ, he thought, he hadn't been married to this girl, had he? By dancing with her in that celebrated parrot dance, he hadn't effectively proposed to her – and been accepted? And now they were off on their honeymoon, without even a best man's speech or a glass of champagne. And with the prospect of bigamy charges to add to his sexual misconduct problems. It was all preposterous of course, but for Brian – for a little while at least – all too possible and all too real. Dancing with bare-breasted young ladies was one thing; walking with them through a forest without a chaperone was quite another, and it was clearly distorting his thoughts. Indeed, only when he and his companions had been loaded back on to their boats – with the young lady in question left on the shore – was he able to return to the world of rational thoughts, and to begin to gird himself against the inevitable comments that would now be made. And they were made; comments that would not allow him to forget that he had been made to look the fool – again – but rather reassuringly by an innocent young girl who had chosen him in preference to a whole rank of unappealing wallflowers (well, that's what he had to tell himself anyway)…

Marriage and mammaries both got a brief mention when dinner got underway, but the conversation soon moved on to less sensitive topics, finally arriving at a discussion as to which categories of people, 'normal' people should feel really sorry for. Those making this judgement were the established team of Linda, Wayne, Angela and William – and of course Brian and Sandra – and it was Wayne who spoke first. For him, amongst those who deserved our sympathy most were the male super-rich residents of the Gulf, grown men who had been robbed by their excessive wealth of any genuinely enriching experiences. All they had were over-designed showy yachts, ghastly ostentatious houses full of ghastly ostentatious furniture, stables of vulgar cars, households of vulgar offspring, the odd private zoo, and no sense of the pride that comes with actually earning the ability to acquire all these possessions. The oil that has made them so wealthy has hollowed out their whole society, and they now lead empty and meaningless lives; lives, Wayne suggested, that are greatly impoverished compared to those of the residents of La Chunga village. And infinitely less laudable.

Heads nodded in agreement around the table, and then Angela put forward her own nomination – which was 'selfie-takers'. Didn't they understand, she said, the corrosive effect of always choosing oneself as the centre of attention? It was a puerile habit that had now graduated to a pernicious disease, and what it would mean for all these selfie-idiots as they grew older – but maybe no wiser – was a concern for us all. Maybe, she suggested, we should feel sorry not for the active selfie-takers of today but for the self-centred, narcissistic idiots they would turn into. A whole global army of Donald Trumps...

Angela found nobody to argue with this nomination – or her concern for the future – and nobody argued with Linda's nomination, which was for cheese-haters. These people, she said, really did warrant our sympathy, because through no fault of their own they had been cut off from one of the most pleasurable experiences available to man, namely the savouring of one or more examples of the almost infinite variety of mankind's greatest achievement: cheese. Sometimes with its second greatest achievement: wine.

That nomination received a small round of applause, at the end of which Sandra put forward her idea, which was that the people we should feel really sorry for were those who pronounced loudly, 'Don't you know who I am!?' There had been so many instances, she said, of prima donnas and various other delusional tosspots who had so lost touch with reality that they really did believe that they deserved special treatment in any situation you could imagine, and could only offer up this affronted, 'Don't you know who I am?' refrain when they failed to receive it. Indeed, this refrain was very telling, because it betrayed the fact that they really believed that whatever their problem was, it arose from a lack of recognition of whom they were and how 'important' they were, and they could not appreciate that it was generally known exactly who they were, just as it was known that they warranted no special treatment whatsoever. They were lost souls, Sandra suggested, people who had let themselves be seduced by their fame or their popularity and could not now deal with life other than through making a complete idiot of themselves. They surely deserved our pity.

Again there were no detractors. Sandra's nomination received total approval. So too, even before he'd really started on his submission, did William's proposal that amongst those for whom we should really feel sorry were creationists. He really didn't have a case to make. After all, who would not feel sorry for a bunch of people who have managed to submerge their combined intellects in a thick soup of idiocy and ignorance? Indeed, he suggested, the only feature that might dent their claim to be deserving of an outpouring of sympathy was their heroic ability to ignore a mountain of evidence that contradicted their views – and the evidence of their own eyes. And that was quite an achievement.

Brian agreed, and in putting forward his own nomination for those deserving our sympathy he borrowed from William's by widening it to encompass all those who had now signed up to cultivating ignorance in all its forms as their lifestyle of choice. They were everywhere, he said. People who think Texas and Hawaii are countries. People who think there is a North Pole but not a South Pole. People who think

Sherlock Holmes was real and Churchill was a myth. And he wasn't making up these examples. They were real, he maintained, along with a thousand others he'd heard that made him wonder what was so unattractive about knowledge that so many people avoided it like the plague. Indeed, it was not, he corrected himself, their antipathy for knowledge that was the problem, but more their positive choice to seek out and embrace ignorance as tightly as they could. It was their badge, something to be proud of – and never something that should make us feel really sorry for them. Even if it most definitely was.

Well, if nothing else, Brian thought that this discussion had certainly exorcised the evil spirit of relations with minors, and he was able to retire to bed confident that in the morning under-clothed young ladies would be yesterday's news and not worthy of mention.

Before then, of course, there was something to mention now – to Sandra – which was his 'what has disappeared from our lives' item for tonight. And on this occasion it was 'toilet chains'.

'Do you remember,' he started, 'the days when all lavatory cisterns were mounted well up on a wall and nowhere near the bowl?'

Sandra was taken aback, but eventually she managed a strained, 'Errh, yes.'

'Right, well apparently what happened was that the loo engineers discovered that they could improve the flushing action in the bowl by improving the waterway design and they therefore didn't need the assistance of gravity that you got from a high-mounted tank.'

'Fascinating.'

'Yes, and of course when you get rid of those elevated cisterns, you also get rid of toilet chains. All you need now is a lever on your low-level cistern, and "pulling the chain" becomes a thing of the past. Toilet chains more or less disappeared overnight.'

'Clearly.'

'But just think,' continued Brian, 'your whole business, say, is making toilet chains – with all those nice wooden and ceramic pulls on them – and one day your finance director presents the next year's budget, and has to point out that there might be a slight problem because the forecast turnover for next year is zero. Nobody wants toilet chains any more, not a single one of them. And the bottom has therefore fallen out of your business.'

'Which might, if you were a major shareholder,' suggested Sandra, 'cause the business to fall out of your bottom.'

Brian screwed up his face. Sandra had usurped his presentation – with a joke of all things. He would have to act fast to retrieve it.

'Very funny,' he offered, 'but if you were that shareholder it would be pretty damn devastating. Although, of course, it has happened before. "Marcellus & Sons Chariots", "The Reliable Drawbridge and Portcullis Corporation" and the much-missed "The Peter and Percy Codpiece Company – by Royal Appointment".'

'But not yet "Brian's Interminable Instructions Inc.".'

That was a stopper. Brian knew his toilet-chain pitch was at an end. Indeed he was almost on the point of telling his wife that she had successfully flushed it away. But instead he settled for an amiable 'goodnight' and turned his attention to a further consideration of the afternoon's encounter with forbidden beauty. In particular, he wondered why he had devoted so much time to evaluating his own reaction to his dance-partner, and so little to what she might have been thinking about him or indeed about the whole experience of having to interact with such very strange strangers. Maybe, it had all been more disconcerting for her than it had been for him.

And maybe a consideration of the feelings of an indigenous youngster might be rather more important than a consideration of the demise of chain-pulls.

Or codpieces, come to that...

16.

rian woke up thinking about food. In particular he was thinking about just how good the food was on his floating conveyance. It was quite simply excellent, and it made him anticipate every meal of the day, even if it happened to be an early-morning breakfast where he and Sandra might find themselves seated next to Mona and Richard. And that is what happened on this new all-at-sea day. Accordingly, when the conversation had consumed the fact that the catamaran had sailed overnight and was now moored off one of the smaller islands of the Pearl Islands Archipelago – and that bacon was a first-class source of tasty nitrites – it all got rather laborious. Mona and Richard were very sweet people and not at all unfriendly. But that said, they just seemed to suck interest out of any verbal exchange and then immediately expel it as unalloyed tedium and dullness. No matter how hard Brian tried to enliven the exchange at the breakfast table, he was frustrated in his aims by a blanket of unresponsiveness edged with a delicate fringe of total indifference. He doubted that either of them could even have spelled 'curiosity'. He also doubted whether he'd ever develop a little empathy and understanding for people unlike himself. Which was all getting a little too serious for such an early hour of the day – and risked getting in the way of his appreciating the quality of the food. So ultimately he focused on that rather than on any more conversation. And it was a good decision. The food was really very good indeed. So too was the rest of the day – in the sense that it was far less than demanding and an ideal preparation for the impending transit of the Panama Canal.

This absence of any pressing demands and the gearing up for some canal time at first manifested themselves in the form of an extended presentation by José on the construction of the Panama Canal – which one could choose to attend or not. Brian and Sandra did, and in this way they soon became further acquainted with the trials and tribulations associated with building one of the world's engineering marvels across the unforgiving terrain of the Panama Isthmus. And it all began, they were told by José, with an English physician and philosopher by the name of Sir Thomas Browne, who speculated in 1668 that 'Some isthmus have been eaten through by the sea and others cut by spade. And if policy would permit, that of Panama in America were most worthy the attempt, it being but a few miles over, and would open a shorter cut unto the East Indies and China'.

Well, the truth of the matter was that Sir TB didn't ever wield a spade himself and he might legitimately be accused of stating the bleedin' obvious – in slightly archaic English. But, there again, the boy had nailed it. He was right on the mark. And it was only a matter of time before somebody or other took up that spade. Even if it was over two hundred years later…

Anyway, it was now time for José to jump forward to 1881, a time when, as Brian and Sandra knew, Panama was a province of Colombia and a time when a French gentleman by the name of Ferdinand de Lesseps was in a position to raise considerable sums that would enable him to embark on the required cross-isthmus canal project. This, of course, was on account of how he'd made a pile by successfully constructing a canal through a desert, otherwise known as the Suez Canal. Unfortunately, however, Ferdinand had achieved only a 'D' in his O-level French history, and he knew barely anything about his own country's mastery of failures. So, he knew sod-all about the French lack of success in the Gallic Wars. Less than sod-all about Agincourt. Sweet Fanny Adams about his country's failure at Trafalgar. Nothing at all about Napoleon's defeat by Wellington. Next to nothing about France's dismal performance in the recent Franco-Prussian War. And of course in the absence of a crystal ball he would have had no knowledge of his native country's pitiful performance in the Second World War or of its repeated failures in the Six Nations rugby tournament. Had he had any idea of how adept his country was in failing so comprehensively and so often, he might have thought twice about taking on this particular canal job. But he didn't, and it wasn't too long before he was notching up yet another notable failure for his all-too-often-failing country. His canal project would prove to be an absolute disaster.

To be fair, the problems he faced were immense, and they included the impenetrability of the rainforests he encountered, the presence in these forests of venomous snakes, insects and spiders, a climate that was desperately enervating, a climate that could quickly render useless his unsophisticated nineteenth-century equipment and, not least by any means, the ravages of debilitating and deadly diseases. On top of all this was his ill-thought-out plan to replicate his Suez success by building a sea-level canal. This was simply fatal to the project. He'd apparently visited the site of the works on only a few occasions, and only in Panama's dry season. He therefore had no idea of the power of the Chagres River (where the canal had been started) in the eight months of the year when it wasn't the dry season, and how what then became a raging torrent made the whole concept of a sea-level canal a complete and literal washout.

So, José concluded, if one is faced with all sorts of venomous critters, impassable vegetation, crappy corroding equipment, an insufferable climate, yellow fever, malaria and various other exotic tropical diseases, and an unsustainable design for one's canal, one soon finds that one has run out of money and one is heading for that next French debacle. Which is not very good news, but arguably it still leaves one better off than the 800,000 French investors who lost all their savings and the 22,000 not necessarily French workers who died as a result of accidents and disease.

Inevitably, Ferdinand called it a day. In fact, he and his son were found guilty of fraud and sentenced to five years in prison – which was ultimately overturned (possibly on the basis that they were merely upholding that ancient French tradition of dismal failure). But that is another story, and it was now time for José to enlighten his audience on the next stage of the principal story, which involved the formation of a second French company to pick up the pieces – and to attempt to comply with the terms of the original concession granted by the Colombians. The manager of this new company was a bloke Brian knew only too well – as he had already given a lecture on him to his companions back at Canopy Tower. Yes, this was Philippe Bunau-Varilla, and Philippe's first smart move was to recognise that a sea-level canal was a non-starter and that what was needed instead was a lock-and-lake canal, a waterway that would use a lock system to raise vessels to a central man-made lake and another lock system to lower them again on the other side – which is exactly how the modern Panama Canal works.

Well, as Brian was well aware, Monsieur Bunau-Varilla was instrumental in securing American involvement in the project – to the extent that they took over the project along with all those preferential rights attaching to the operation of the canal and the control of the land through which the canal would run. And so on May 4 1904 the Yanks arrived, and inherited from the French a severely depleted workforce, a mishmash of buildings, infrastructure and kit (much of it in very poor condition) – and a Herculean task. Indeed; the task was so overwhelming it… overwhelmed the first guy appointed to oversee it, and this led to another guy by the name of John Frank Stevens being recruited, and he took over the mantle in 1905.

He was a Mister Sensible, and the first thing he focused on was the needs of the workforce that would actually build the canal. So rather than cracking on with clearance and excavation stuff, he devoted most of his energies to building and rebuilding all the housing, hotels, cafeterias, repair shops and warehouses that the project would require – along with sorting out all the infrastructure that the thousands of incoming workers would require. He then began to recruit these workers, enticing all those people he would need from the US and elsewhere with the promise of not just good pay but also the sort of accommodation and environment that would enable them to live in reasonable safety and comfort. He also, very importantly, re-established the cross-isthmus railway that he knew would be vital to the construction process. Only with an upgraded functioning railway would he be able to shift the millions of tons of soil that would be excavated from the mountains to the dam he would build across the Chagres River, in order to create his Panama Canal lake.

This was all good stuff, but being Mister Sensible he knew he would still have a huge problem with malaria and yellow fever. Accordingly, a military gentleman by the name of Colonel William C Gorgas was appointed as the project's chief sanitation officer. By this time, of course, it was well understood how malaria, yellow fever and many other tropical diseases were mosquito borne. So Colonel Will soon got stuck into all sorts of… well, sanitation measures. And these included the provision of modern water systems, the fumigation of buildings, the spraying of insect-breeding areas with oil and larvicide, the elimination of stagnant water and, according to José, the replacement of medicated toilet paper with the infinitely preferable soft variety. There again, José was grinning like an idiot when he recounted this last measure implemented by Colonel Will, and Brian was not at all convinced it was true. What was true, however, was that after two years of concerted effort, this US military hero had succeeded in almost eliminating mosquito-spread diseases. Even so, José went on to explain (now without a grin on his face), 5,600 workers died of diseases and accidents during the US construction work. And whilst this was a very significant improvement on the record of the French, it still represented a terrible cost in human life – and, of course, an end to life for all those who made up the statistic.

Anyway, José, at this stage of his presentation, took his audience back to the commencement of the project and to the fact that in 1905, a sea-level canal was still being recommended by a US engineering panel as the optimum design. And it wasn't until 1906, after Stevens had observed the Chagres River in full flood, that he announced on a visit to Washington that a sea-level approach would be 'an entirely untenable proposition'. He argued in favour of a canal with a lock system that would raise and lower ships to and from a large reservoir eighty-five feet above sea level. This would be the man-made Gaton Lake (the largest man-made lake in the world at that time) and it would be created by building the Gatun Dam – which would be the largest dam in the world at that time. Mr Stevens, it appears, not only didn't lack confidence but he also wasn't to be found wanting in respect of his no doubt oversized *cojones*. And, of course, he knew he was right.

Well, it was now time for José to impress his audience with some figures. The first of these was the 170,000,000 cubic yards of soil that had to be excavated over and above the 30,000,000 cubic yards excavated by the French. As quickly as possible the Americans had replaced or upgraded the old French equipment with new equipment designed for the much larger scale of construction, and this had included the introduction of about 100 new large railroad-mounted steam shovels – which were significantly bigger than spades. Add in new huge steam-powered cranes, giant hydraulic rock crushers, pneumatic drills, concrete mixers and dredgers, and one would soon arrive at the end of the construction process and some final José-supplied figures. Yes, despite Mr Stevens resigning as chief engineer as early as 1907 and being replaced by a US Army major by the name of George Washington Goethals, the work on the canal was successfully concluded in 1914 – a full two years ahead of schedule – and it was formally opened on August 15, 1914. And it had cost, José proudly announced, a trifling $500,000,000 – which is roughly equivalent to just over $12,000,000,000 in today's money. Which, thought Brian, for such a remarkable feat of engineering didn't sound too much at all. And anyway, they'd have saved an awful lot of money if, despite what José had claimed, they had in fact stuck with the medicated toilet paper…

Brian had listened with interest to all that José had said. However, this presenter of the lecture wasn't quite finished, because he hadn't yet said a word about the 'Panama Canal expansion project'. Well, now he did, and he started by telling his audience that despite opinions to the contrary, size really did matter, especially when the size in question was the size of yer locks. Yes, mammoth though the original Panama Canal was, it wasn't anywhere near mammoth enough to accommodate the new generation of super-mammoth cargo ships. These were one-and-a-half times the size of the biggest ships that could navigate the original canal, and could carry twice as much cargo. And there were more and more of these super-heavyweights – many of them looking to take goods from China to the East coast and Gulf coast of America, and looking also for a bigger Panama Canal that could accommodate their size. They weren't that keen on sailing around the tip of Cape Horn.

It was therefore inevitable that Panama would commit itself to building two new sets of locks – one each on the Atlantic and Pacific sides of the canal – that would turn the current two-lane waterway into a three-lane route through the country. But of more importance would be the size of these locks. In contrast to the existing locks which were a mere thirty-three metres wide, 320 metres long and twelve-and-a-half metres deep, these new beasties would be a massive fifty-five metres wide, 427 metres long and eighteen metres deep. That would mean that with some associated widening and deepening of the canal's channels, the new Panama Canal would be able to handle not just 45% of the world's cargo-carrying vessels but almost 80%, even if they were packed to their inscrutable gunnels.

Credit has to go to the Panama authorities for putting the decision to embark on this super-expensive, highly disruptive expansion project to a national referendum. But they did – in 2006 – and it won the overwhelming approval of the population. Accordingly, construction of the new locks began in 2007 with the intention of it being finalised in 2014, the 100th anniversary of the opening of the original canal. Unfortunately, this didn't happen. Strikes, disputes, arguments over cost overruns and too many equality and diversity training courses pushed out the completion date, and the new facilities were not opened until June 2016. However, when they were they not only worked but they began to recoup their cost straightaway. As José was keen to point out – with another of his figures – the Panama Canal now earns a cool $1.2 million every time it is used by the biggest of ships. And as every good housewife knows, if one looks after the millions the billions soon look after themselves, and everybody with a stake in the Panama Canal ends up as happy as Larry. And so too do the Chinese – until, that is, they get around to building even bigger ships. At which point they might have to remove Panama completely, and probably without any compunction whatsoever…

Strangely enough, the Chinese featured again over lunch. José's dissertation on the Canal had now drawn to a conclusion and Brian and Sandra had been drawn to the lunch table, where they were joined by the four Germans on board. They all, of course, had a facility with English, and Dieter (of Dieter and Erica) first used this facility to inform Brian and Sandra that he and his wife were from Dresden. Neither Brian nor Sandra knew how to acknowledge this revelation without displaying some very obvious English guilt, but Stephan (of Stephan and Tilda) came to their aid by sharing with his table companions something he'd recently read concerning the Chinese, and in particular their ambitions in space. And what he'd read was that they planned to land a robotic probe of some sort on the far side of the moon. This initiated a conversation that would not have been welcomed by President Xi or by any other of those expressionless mannequins who run the country. To begin with, Tilda pointed out in perfect English that it was quite ironic that a country busily engaged in depleting one world of its natural treasures should be expending its energies on another that had none of these at all. After a number of similar contributions from around the table, Brian concluded this anti-Chinese episode by wondering out loud whether anybody had thought to tell the Chinese that they were very unlikely to find any elephants on the dark side of the moon – or even a stash of old ivory.

Lunch concluded, it was time for a boat trip to examine at close quarters that ancient abandoned submarine – which was on a nearby island – or, if one was so inclined, to soak up the pleasures afforded by a beautiful catamaran parked off a beautiful island in the Tropics. No prizes for guessing what Brian and Sandra did, although in the interests of fairness it should be pointed out that a little reading was undertaken – nowhere near the bar – and it wasn't until a respectable 6.45 that they equipped themselves with a couple of G&Ts. When challenged by

Wayne to explain why this was such a popular drink for Brits both at home and abroad, Brian put forward two reasons. One was that it was one of the most deliciously refreshing drinks imaginable. The other was that it enabled his wife and himself to mourn the passing of all those other G&Ts in modern spoken English. And when asked to explain what he meant by this, Brian informed his Canadian friend that all too often in England these days, one did not hear – even on the BBC – something like 'he's fitting in a meeting this morning', but instead the G&T denuded ''e's fi-in' in a mee-in' this mornin''. And, Brian went on to say, for him and for many of his fellow middle-aged grumps this was all very upse-in'.

In fact, it was a great deal more upsetting than the prospect of dinner with the three Americans on the catamaran with whom he and Sandra had, up to now, had only minimal dealings. These were the mismatched American couple and the singleton American lady as already alluded to, and this evening they would be Brian and Sandra's sole table companions for this, the last meal of the day. Now, the only reason that they might be the cause of any upset at all was twofold. In the case of the 'mismatches' this was merely because the male of this pair, Geoffrey, was clearly in his sixties and his female partner with whom he was sharing a cabin (Brenda) was, in purely arithmetic terms, young enough to be his granddaughter. She could have been no more than twenty-five. As regards the singleton, middle-aged American, Rhona, it was a very different matter. Her potential-upset credentials lay in her habit of telling anyone who would listen to her how she had done anything one could imagine and could easily top anything you might have done – in spades. Brian had already learnt not ask her any questions and never to be alone in her company.

Well, as Brian would never have predicted, the dinner went swimmingly. Geoffrey had clearly formed the same opinion of Rhona as had Brian, and he joined forces with Brian and Sandra to curtail her intrusion into any conversation to great effect. She was very politely muzzled and was not able to dominate a single topic of conversation with yet another Rhona story of achievement. Furthermore, Geoffrey was very open with his new table companions and lost no time in telling them that having divorced his first wife forty years previously (after one terrible year of marriage) he had now found himself a girlfriend, and he and Brenda were sharing a vacation that had already taken them to Colombia and may or may have not taken them into the world of carnal knowledge. All that could be said with certainty is that intimacy must have played some part in their relationship because conversation certainly did not. Brenda, in strictly empirical terms, was dumb, and would only utter (a few) words in response to a direct question.

Nevertheless, even with one essentially silent diner at the table and another who was being actively constrained, it proved a memorable and enjoyable meal – at least for Brian. After opening up about his failed marriage and his successful new relationship with a woman, Geoffrey provided his companions with the information that he had spent his working life with

Boeing and, although now retired, was an aeroplane man through and through. This was really good news in that Brian and Sandra were both plane nuts themselves. Both of them were known to drool over pictures of Vulcans and Harriers, and neither of them had any problem at all in discussing all sorts of military and commercial aeroplanes with Geoffrey – well into the main course. In fact, the only slight error that either of them made was when Brian introduced Concorde into the conversation, and how this represented an unmatched pinnacle in the history of aeronautical engineering. It wasn't the wisest thing to say to a Boeing man, but to Geoffrey's credit he didn't react too badly at all. He just glared for a few seconds.

Anyway, one cannot live on planes alone, and in due course the conversation moved on to some more predictable (middle-aged) topics, in which even Rhona could make a contribution (but not Brenda). The first was the dearth of decent new films. Where, Geoffrey asked, had all the good film-makers gone, and why rather than dozens of new classics were we now expected to live on a diet of poor remakes, yet another *Fast and Furious* bowl of slop, another warmed-up leftover in the *Pirates of the Caribbean* franchise, or some no-dialogue, all-action, CGI-soaked, comic-book load of nonsense? Sandra responded to this question by suggesting that risk-taking, creativity and imagination were all now rare commodities in the film industry, and it was far easier for all those big corporations that now ran this industry to make their money from a combination of undemanding trash and a never-ending series of interminable television box-sets, which themselves were more mesmerising than demanding. Brian and Rhona agreed – but Brenda said nothing. Nor did she utter a word when Brian moved the conversation on to a new topic – which concerned the literal devaluation of academic achievements in Britain that he'd moaned about before…

You see, he'd now worked out that with one in eight of the UK population presently being regarded as capable of earning a first-class degree, it would soon be possible to populate the twenty largest provincial cities in the UK with just first-class degree holders. The whole of Birmingham, Leeds, Manchester, Sheffield, Glasgow, Bradford and fourteen other major British conurbations could be stuffed with outsized intellects, and all those managing just second- and third-class degrees (along with a dwindling minority who had collected no degree at all) could be stored away in the countryside and in the country's capital – which so richly deserved them. When he aired this result of his latest calculations, his only challenge came from his wife and it was in the form of her suggesting that it was quite possible that he would have to revise his calculations when it was judged that the awarding of anything less than a first-class degree would be regarded as an infringement of one's human rights. In which case, even London would have to learn to accommodate some intellect. So, all that remained for him to do was to enjoy the rest of his meal and give just a little bit of thought to what might be his 'what has gone from our lives' subject for the evening. This he did, so that when back in their cabin, he was able to share with Sandra that tonight the subject of his talk would be 'optimism'.

This was a bit different to budgies in cages, bob-a-job-week and Allen Scythes but, he assured his wife, it was certainly something that had disappeared from many people's lives. The default position for most was now unrelenting pessimism and it was unlikely that any degree of optimism would return in the foreseeable future, if indeed ever.

'Just think,' he said to Sandra, 'when we were young the world was overflowing with optimism. It was everywhere. It was in science, in space exploration, in widening horizons, in music and in our everyday experience. Things just seemed to be getting better all the time, and pessimism didn't see the light of day. It was locked away in a box along with guilt, stress, anguish and regret. But then something happened, something that started to temper that optimism and then to remove it entirely…'

'We realised we were screwing up the world,' interrupted an apparently engaged Sandra.

'Yeah, and we began to realise that the world was full of malign forces, some of them intent on blowing us up, and others intent on simply reducing the world to a pretty unpleasant place – full of bondage, suffering, corruption and abuse. And we, on our little island off the coast of Europe, seemed to be more and more under threat, and more and more not in control. The world was beginning to press in, at the same time as it was being degraded by the weight of a burgeoning mankind. And then, of course, there was that painful slow death – of any decent comedy on the telly…'

'Jesus, Brian, you sure know how to cheer a girl up…'

But he didn't really. Not enough to put pessimism back in that box. Although with the impending transit through the canal, he might just be able to lift the lid a little to let out a bit of anticipation. And who could tell? Tomorrow might even see pessimism overwhelmed for a few hours by some genuine childlike joy. Who wouldn't be excited or even enthralled by a close encounter with one of the greatest feats of engineering ever? Hell, thought Brian, even Brenda might exclaim her delight!

17.

*N*orm hadn't organised the building of a new Coca-Cola plant in Russia, but his wife, Hailey, had. Together they constituted the 'fit-looking American couple' first identified by Brian when he'd stepped aboard the *Discovery*, and right now they were sharing a breakfast table with him and with Sandra. It was the first opportunity either of them had had to have a proper chat with them, but not the first opportunity to judge that they were undoubtedly trim in their appearance and much younger-looking than they probably were. They just exuded vitality. Especially the creator of bottling plants in foreign parts, a woman who had clearly been gifted with more than her fair share of ever-lasting genes. There was no doubt about it, thought Brian; the day would come when she and her handsome side-kick husband would both be sought by the purveyors of pension products and the like to tout their wares. They would be harnessed to appear in countless TV adverts, all of them gilding the reality of unwelcome old age by this pair's carefully-crafted appearance on cruise ships, on the sunlit terraces of some *very nice* hotels, and on some undemanding cliff-top walks (with or without a golden retriever). And all the time they would be smiling and looking so satisfied with themselves, having of course had the sense to invest in such a good pension product as well as the unspoken good fortune not to have arrived in old age with either Zimmer frames or any obvious signs of ageing (other than maybe some silver-white hair set above Norm's improbably smooth face).

In fact, as he sat at the breakfast table, Brian began to wonder whether he should offer to become their agent, the man who would optimise their earnings from all those inevitable adverts. And to start with, maybe he should get some head-shots, some photos of their unlined highly photogenic faces to act as their calling card. And where better than where they were now: back in the Panama City marina. Yes, overnight, the *Discovery* had abandoned the Pearl Islands in favour of a mooring in the very spot from where she'd sailed away just three days before. And this meant that Brian's two new clients could be photographed with directly behind them that incredible Panama City skyline. And how effective would that be? Drama to add to their undeniable Peter Pan qualities. And this would make them completely irresistible to any number of producers of the relevant commercials…

Unfortunately, it wasn't to be. Brian's ideas were somehow overtaken by his admiration for anybody who could put together a working factory in Putin-land – and then the *Discovery* weighed anchor. Even before Brian had initiated his toothpick assault on the morsels of toast between his teeth, the catamaran was on the move and the view of Panama City was becoming obscured by other vessels. And soon after this, it had disappeared entirely – to be replaced with a view of the beginning of the Panama Canal!

Brian was outside now, with Sandra and all of the *Discovery's* passengers. Quite clearly none of them intended to miss a second of what would be their first encounter with this engineering marvel – even if it was still quite difficult to see where this marvel began. It was all on such a large scale, and although they all knew that they were now looking at the Pacific mouth of the Panama Canal, it wasn't before they were approaching the huge 'Bridge of the Americas' that they knew they were on target for the canal's first locks and the Panama Canal proper.

This bridge is an elegant cantilever construction, and one of just two bridges that keep the two 'halves' of Panama connected. It hadn't really occurred to Brian before, but of course if you drive a ruddy great canal through the centre of your country, you divide your country into two bits, and those bits really do need to be kept together. Otherwise you might end up with a Pan and a completely separate Ama, with anti-Ama and anti-Pan sentiments quickly developing on respective sides – and then even the prospect of Pan-versus-Ama hostilities breaking out. And this, of course, would result in complete panamademonium for the world's shipping industry.

Fortunately, there seems little likelihood of this, as long as the Bridge of the Americas (together with its sister bridge further along the canal) continues to shift traffic between the two halves of the country.

Furthermore, the bridge acts as a link while at the same time allowing almost all the world's cruise ships to use the canal. Clearance under its main span is just over 200 feet, which means that only the biggest floating hotels such as the *Oasis of the Seas* and the *Harmony of the Seas* cannot squeeze beneath it. Apparently, whilst they can fit into the canal's widened locks they are too tall for the bridge. Which, Brian decided, might not be a bad thing.

Anyway, it wasn't long before the *Discovery* was passing under the bridge (with lots of headroom to spare) and on its right appeared Balboa Port. This, José told all those within earshot, was now the busiest container port in Latin America. And it certainly contained lots of… containers, and it housed some of the biggest container cranes Brian had ever seen – all painted in a rather nice shade of green.

This facility held the attention of all those on board for quite some time. (There was a large container ship there currently being loaded with containers.) However, the combined attention of the *Discovery's* passengers eventually shifted to the first set of locks of the Panama Canal, otherwise known as the Miraflores Locks. To start with there wasn't much to see: just a long, low agglomeration of 'stuff' beneath a small forest of giant lampposts. But then the stuff began to resolve itself into the obvious shapes of gargantuan locks. First there was the new single set of locks that catered for the very largest of ships – and this was currently empty. And then there were the two sets of original locks, and going into the left-hand one of these was a sizeable cargo ship called the *Sea Breeze*. It wasn't the biggest ship in the world, but compared to the *Discovery* it was enormous. Oh, and, according to José, it would be sharing the lock with a small 'day ferry' that was on its way to Gatun Lake – and with the *Discovery*. These old 'smaller' locks were still quite big enough to accommodate three vessels: one large one at the front and two smaller ones side by side at the rear.

Blimey! It was beginning to dawn on Brian why this canal had taken years to build and why it really was an engineering wonder of the world. It was all so bloody colossal.

Inserting the *Discovery* into the lock was a captivating experience, not least because this modest-sized catamaran had to wait for the day ferry to arrive to take its place in the lock first. And while it waited its skipper had stationed it not far from the exit of the parallel set of locks, down which was coming another mammoth ship. This meant that the *Discovery's* passengers could see the huge white superstructure of this ship towering above a set of lock gates – and, if so inclined, they could try to calculate the weight of water and maritime metal that was currently suspended above them. Nothing was likely to go wrong in any way, but it was still a little intimidating to be such a small thing as a human in the presence of so much that was so much bigger – and so much above one. Or at least Brian thought so anyway.

Indeed, he felt more than happy when it was finally time for the catamaran's skipper to move it out of the 'wrong lane' and take it along the right (left) lane and into the first of the Miraflores locks. This gentleman, in Brian's view, often looked as though he suffered from acute consternation, but he was obviously extremely composed and more than proficient. Accordingly, he completed the required manoeuvre with practised skill, and without hitting either of the vessels that were already there. So, very soon, Brian was able to exchange waved pleasantries with the passengers on the ferry (just feet away) and examine the back of the cargo ship at very close quarters. And then the lock gates behind the *Discovery* began to close…

Wow! Brian decided the word was 'majestic'. Here were two 'doors' coming together to form a barrier that would withstand the pressure exerted by 22,000,000 imperial gallons of water (the amount required to fill this first of the Miraflores locks). And to do that job one could not rely on something made of wood. No, one had to put in place eighty-foot tall metal lock gates that are seven feet thick and each of which weighs in at nearly 700 tons. When operated, these hollow gates begin to fill with water as they close, and ultimately each of them locks in place with its partner to form a 'V' shape pointing upstream. This way the force of the water from the higher side pushes the ends of the gates together and makes for a near-perfect seal. The gates can then only be opened again when, at the end of the operating cycle, the water level on both sides is equal.

It was a super-impressive sight, not least because it all worked so well – and apparently so easily. As José explained, the gates are so well balanced that it takes only very small motors to move them – and the gates are by no means modern in their design. In fact, as far as Brian could tell, they are the gates that have been in service for decades, if not the original gates in use when the canal was first commissioned. They certainly looked pretty ancient, with a sheet-metal and multiple rivet construction that Isambard Kingdom Brunel would have recognised (or maybe even regarded as a little old-fashioned).

Anyway, they did their job superbly, and after less than ten minutes the *Discovery*, together with its two floating companions, was well above the level of the Pacific, and ready to enter the second chamber of the Miraflores Locks. Just as soon, that is, as the freighter and the ferry had shifted along.

For the ferry, this would involve the use of its engines. For the much larger freighter, it would involve not just the use of its engines but also the employment of a team of mules. No, not that sort, but little electric motor 'mules' which run along a set of tracks on either side of the locks. They are no less than vital, as whilst a large ship can move forward under its own power, it needs some side-to-side guidance – and some braking control – which is what is supplied by these dinky little silver engines. After all, the clearance between the sides of most of these large ships and the lock walls is tiny. Often, one couldn't even slip an MP's humility between the two of them. So these mules are essential, as is the skill of their operators, highly-trained mule-drivers who, through cables linking their machines to the ships, are able to nurse these vessels through and then set them on their way.

The *Sea Breeze* needed four of these mules, one each side at its bow, and one each side at its stern. And as the freighter moved forward, Brian could see that as the mules moved forward with it, their drivers were using winches within their vehicles to take the cables in or to play them out in order to keep the vessel centred in the lock chamber and its paintwork intact. It was mesmerising: an intricate mechanical ballet of sorts, but with forces at work that would flatten most ballet venues – and with performers at work who were probably on a bonus scheme and wore work boots and jeans (and thought a *grande jeté* must be something like Balboa port, and not something like Southend Pier as Brian had thought).

Well, the ballet was concluded, and the three patient craft were now positioned within the second chamber of the Miraflores Locks. It was therefore time to close the second set of lock gates, this set being a double set, put there to guard against a possible gate failure. This was highly unlikely, but it could happen as a result of a runaway ship, and if the gates were breached it would probably lead to some catastrophic flooding of the land downstream and several years of employment for a team of lawyers. Consequently, the builders of the canal provided two pairs of gates at each of the upper chambers of each flight of locks – and an even more impressive sight for the passengers of the *Discovery* as a doubled-up tonnage of ironwork began to close behind them to seal off the lock. And, of course, the two pairs of gates closed in practised synchronised solidarity. It was a joy to behold.

So too was the sight of the *Sea Breeze* steaming out of the lock into Miraflores Lake. The lock chamber had been filled, the twin set of gates at its head had been opened, and the mules had forsaken their hold on their charge, which was now well on its way to... the next set of locks at the other end of Miraflores Lake. The skipper of the ferry and the skipper of the *Discovery* lost no time in following the bigger vessel, and after only a few minutes it was time for all three of them to organise themselves for admission into the Pedro Miguel Locks, the last locks on this Pacific side of the canal that would let them into the 'Gaillard Cut' and eventually into Gatun Lake.

Well, the Pedro Miguel Locks were no less fascinating than their Miraflores counterparts – albeit, they were a single step and not a double step. There was just one enormous lock chamber and not two – although, of course, it not being able to avoid being an upper chamber, it had two pairs of gates at each end – and twice the delight for the *Discovery's* passengers. It also gave them their first canal-based view of the Centennial Bridge.

This is the bridge that was built to relieve the traffic pressure on the Bridge of the Americas – and to provide a passage over the canal for Brian and Sandra when they were still in the motoring stage of their Panama holiday. Driving over it had been quite exciting for them, but seeing it from canal level and then passing under it was really quite thrilling. Yes, the Pedro Miguel Locks had now been successfully negotiated, and the *Discovery* was in the Cut and sailing under the elegant 'cable-stayed' construction that was Panama's Centennial Bridge and its second route across the canal – and its highest (it clears the canal by a little more than 260 feet). And that meant it was time to have a number of close encounters – of the weird kind...

It was the mega-ships coming down the Gaillard Cut on their way to the Pacific, floating behemoths moving silently down this huge incision through the guts of Panama to return to their natural home on the wide-open seas. And in the case of most of them that came by, to return to their ports of origination somewhere in Asia. The first was the *Yang Ming Insurgence*, a huge container ship which, assuming it was of Chinese origin, didn't impress Brian with its owner's choice of name. Maybe something along the lines of *YM Friendship* or even *YM Nosegay* might have struck a less threatening chord. Then it was the *Aegean Highway* which, given that its home port was advertised as Kobe, didn't say much about Japanese knowledge of geography. It didn't say much about their appreciation of aesthetics either. The *Aegean Highway* was a grey-coloured lump designed to carry hundreds of motor cars from the land of the rising sun to the lands of the permanently sinking sun – and it was about as attractive as a slightly chamfered breezeblock. One couldn't even distract oneself by doing a container count – which was possible on the next three ships as well as on the *YM Insurgence*. All four lent themselves to a little bit of tallying and a little bit of mental-arithmeticking in order to calculate just how many hundreds or thousands of containers they were carrying – that were visible – to add to the however many more were accommodated below. Having done a couple of calculations, it seemed to Brian that the world was somehow engaged in an absurd exercise of transporting far too much stuff from X to Y, when it would be much better – especially for the world – if

Y returned to making the stuff for itself and let X get on with learning that killing elephants and whales really wasn't such a good idea.

Brian even thought he might broadcast these views to those aboard these oriental hulks in the vain hope that they might take his lesson of enlightenment back to their own shores. But it was never going to happen, not least because he saw not a single person on any of these passing monsters. He had read that they had very small crews – in number, not necessarily stature terms – but he had not realised that the very few people who sailed them across the seas were never in view. And why would they be? They could hardly shuffle the containers around by hand, and they had far more important jobs to do 'indoors' – like navigating the ship, heating up the noodles for dinner or playing just one further game of *Grand Theft Auto 2*. What Nelson's men would have made of these modern mariners, Brian shuddered to think, but eventually he decided that if they were in a fix it would be (probably literally) mincemeat.

Anyway, Brian's thoughts were eventually captured by the appearance on the right side of the Cut of the *Titan* floating crane, the crane he had first seen during his stay at Canopy Tower. Because the *Discovery* was now approaching the end of the Cut – as evidenced by the appearance of the Gamboa Bridge that spans the Chagres River, and over which Brian and Sandra had been driven to the Soberania National Park. They were now in known territory again, and since they had last been here, Brian had learnt a great deal more about that Chagres River.

He now knew, for example, that it was the very key to the functioning of the Panama Canal. It, all on its own, fed the man-made lake that served as the reservoir for the entire canal system. And this was crucial. After all, even with some clever engineering that effectively recycled some of the water in the chambers of the new, larger locks, an awful lot of water was needed to fill all three lock systems. And once used, this water would be flushed into either the Pacific or the Caribbean, and the only winners from this disposable-water system would be some frigate birds and the like. (They linger around the Pacific and Caribbean ends of the canal on the lookout for freshwater fish that have been flushed into salt water when the locks are emptied – and that soon become terminally distressed.)

So... if the Chagres River doesn't continue to flow, the Panama Canal will not continue to operate. Which might be very good news for the wilderness of east Panama (including Darién). Quite simply, if the forest cover in this area is degraded it is quite likely that rainfall patterns will be severely disrupted, and without the rain, the Chagres River will not flow, and certainly not nearly enough to feed all those hungry locks. For once, thought Brian, a bit of large-scale man-made engineering might prove the saviour of a chunk of nature. And ironically, all those eager-beaver ships from East Asia might be playing their own unintended part in this very welcome preservation of the planet. It made Brian smile – just before he smiled even more when the *Discovery* completed its transit of the Gaillard Cut and entered the extensive and beautifully framed waters of Gatun Lake.

It really was quite stunning and, as part of a canal, about as un-canal-like as it was possible to be. It was an inland sea, surrounded by unspoilt tree-covered slopes and studded with unspoilt tree-covered islands. It made for a memorable bit of cruising for all the *Discovery's* passengers – and an ideal situation to park up for the rest of the day. Yes, the *Discovery* had been given the rare privilege of being allowed to moor on Gatun Lake for the rest of the day and overnight, and its fortunate complement of travellers could now indulge themselves in food, drink and banter for as long as they liked and in the certain knowledge that they could enjoy an undisturbed night thereafter – in one of the most remarkable stretches of water in the world.

This hedonistic phase of the trip started with a sea-food barbeque consumed on the upper deck of the *Discovery*, and was followed by a lazy, not-entirely-teetotal afternoon in preparation for a not-necessarily-teetotal evening. It was just that sort of place: a little sybaritic sanctuary from the good sense and good practice of everyday life, somewhere that afforded one of those rare opportunities to be one's careless self rather than being one's normal careful and cautious self. And what did Brian do with this heaven-sent break? When dinner time arrived, he harangued his evening-meal table companions with his thoughts on the greatest threats that currently faced the world…

He wasn't on his normal 'over-population/species extinction as a result' soapbox here, but on the threats posed to our present world order – or, more precisely, the survival of the enlightened Western world against all those who were seeking to destroy it. Anyway, he launched his latest ill-considered assault in the form of a question, and this question was a very simple 'what presents the major threat to our existence?' When all that this question did was cause a series of puzzled looks around the dinner table, he then explained that what he had in mind was a discussion of the threats posed to modern Western mankind – other than the attempt by some gender-super-sensitive idiots to rephrase this question with a reference to humanity rather than mankind.

His puzzled-looking audience on this occasion was Linda and Wayne, Norm and Hailey, and of course his beloved wife Sandra – who currently wasn't expressing her belovedness through her facial expression. In fact, she looked a little vexed, if not latently incensed. Probably because she had seen her husband on these sorts of manoeuvres before, and she knew where it would inevitably lead: into another of his interminable monologues. And unfortunately, she was right. In the absence of any immediate answer to his question, he proceeded to answer it himself.

'Well,' he started, 'Russia is an obvious candidate, isn't it? A belligerent, nuclear-armed, anti-Western state, complete with a chip on its shoulder – and a state that's been spoiling for a fight for years. And as our resolve fades and theirs grows by the day, a time must surely come when they'll try their chance. Probably while our old mucker, Trump, is still in office and before Putin runs out of legitimacy entirely, even with his own downtrodden peasants at home…'

This opening statement changed a couple of puzzled looks at the table into ones of alarm, but nobody said anything, and Brian carried on.

'Well, I think not. Russia can't even make a domestic toaster that anybody wants. The idea of it making a success out of some sort of strike on the West is nothing less than absurd. I mean, Russia is rotten. It's run by gangsters for the benefit of other gangsters, and at the expense of the supremely supine Russian people. And that is not the sort of nation that can achieve anything at all – unless, of course, it cheats. And whilst you can cheat at sport, and cheat the odd individual out of life with polonium or some other noxious substance, you cannot cheat in a conventional confrontation with other countries. Even Europe on its own would probably be more than a match for Russia. It would just have to bombard it with toasters…'

At this point, Norm made a mistake. If Russia wasn't the major threat, he asked, who was?

Brian smiled and then answered Norm's question.

'Well, not China.'

Norm looked surprised.

'China's very different to Russia – and much, much more competent. On top of that I'll concede that China is the world's super-power-in-waiting and that very soon it will be not just an economic giant but a military one as well. And if it chose to, it could snuff out our flame on a whim. However… if George Orwell was still with us today, he would have spotted that China's golden future may be more fool's gold than real…'

'Meaning?' encouraged Norm.

'Well, China is apparently very busy implementing a "social credit" system. And in very rough terms what this means is that it's now using a combination of "big data", recognition technology and artificial intelligence to create a comprehensive system of political and social control, which will make Big Brother look like an amateur. I mean, it's already happening. Anybody deemed to be acting in an anti-social manner – by protesting, say, or maybe just by jay-walking – will be captured by surveillance cameras and will then find that their "social credit" has been reduced, and they then can't buy a train ticket or maybe get a mortgage. Everybody's behaviour will be monitored all the time, except maybe if they happen to belong to the Communist party – and only by behaving very well (in the eyes of Mr Xi's party) will they be able to lead a normal life. Or at least what passes for a normal life in China. Rigid control of everybody's life is already becoming a reality…'

'And?' encouraged Norm again.

'And I predict it will blow up in their face, well before they suffocate the rest of the world – including us. I mean, even the Chinese have got their limits, and being reduced to the status of an automaton, required to perform in a predetermined manner – by a load of gits who look like automatons – is going to be far too much for them to bear. There'll eventually be a revolt, a big one. And when this happens China will go backwards so fast it might actually slip off the planet. And even if it doesn't it will be in no position to threaten the West.'

It was time for Sandra to make her presence known, and she did this with a carefully enunciated and pointed question.

'Brian,' she said, 'I'm guessing you have now completed the fanciful part of your presentation, and can we all hope that the rest of your presentation is both a little shorter and a little less fanciful?'

Brian responded immediately.

'Mark Zuckerberg. He's the greatest threat.'

'Greater than Russia and China?' asked Hailey.

'Yes. Social media is toxic. It is already poisoning the minds of an entire generation, and the dose is so large that it will no doubt soon prove fatal to the whole of Western society – and much sooner than anybody thinks. You cannot infantilise, patronise, mislead, distract, abuse and hold captive literally hundreds of millions of people without the societies these people represent falling to pieces. It won't need a first nuclear strike or a giant Chinese army to obliterate the West, but just some more screen time and then some more – along with a continued stream of Presidential tweets. We're screwed, my friends – by Mr Zuckerberg and his high-tech henchmen – and there's nothing we can do to stop him.'

Well, Brian readied himself for an assault. He had certainly earned one. But it didn't come. Instead, all he got was a series of nodding heads. Even Sandra was nodding her agreement with his denouement! Crikey, had he known it would be this easy, he'd have picked a different topic, something along the lines of the moral justification for the indefinite incarceration of repeat offenders. But hey. He'd at least confirmed that he wasn't the only still-sane geyser on the planet, even if he was one of a severely endangered species. Long live the real world, he thought, and down with Zuckerberg and his screens…

Anyway, Sandra's behaviour had won her a little reprieve. When back in their cabin, he announced that the latest chapter of his 'what has disappeared from our lives' treatise would be held over to tomorrow evening. Although, of course, that did mean that she would then have to manage two in one go. She didn't seem to mind. Maybe she saw the reprieve as very good news – and was banking on the possibility of Western civilisation having come to an end well before tomorrow evening.

It was a false hope. Moored here on this fabulous Gatun Lake, isolated from the rest of the world, they would probably never have known that the Western world had come to an end. To start with, neither of them had unpacked their phones…

18.

reakfast was just a little bit of a trial for Brian's table companions who, this morning, comprised William and Angela, Wayne and Linda – and Sandra. It started off badly with one of his dreadfully contrived questions, which was to ask whether having an ornamental shoulder-piece attached to your military uniform would constitute an epaulettic fit. It then went from bad to worse when Brian made an observation about William's consumption of a banana and Sandra's application onto her toast of some jam – before dealing with her own banana. William, Brian had learnt, lived in Washington state but was born in Alabama. So, he observed out loud, on 'a small Panama Canal catamaran, an Alabama man had a small banana and Sandra had what was a Panama Canal jam *and* a small banana'. That was forty-two 'a's in a row without the use of any other vowels and, in Brian's mind, well worthy of a round of applause and even a pair of honorary epaulettes. But all he got was a chorus of groans and some advice from Sandra concerning the use of his mouth for eating rather than for talking. It wasn't really a surprise. He knew very well that these were simply the sort of reactions that brilliance often evokes. He would have to leave it to his biographers to recognise his genius and his wit. And meanwhile he'd just have a banana himself.

What he wouldn't have – directly after breakfast – was a ride in a kayak. This was an activity on offer for all those aboard the *Discovery*, but for Brian – and for Sandra – it was a not very attractive offer. In the first place, it was steaming hot and none of the kayaks were of the coupé variety that might provide some shade from the sun. In the second place, it was announced that all those committing themselves to a water-borne slipper should not go too close to the nearby island as it was a popular hang-out place for crocs! Unbelievable – and not the sort of thing one would expect on the Grand Union Canal. Or indeed on most of the world's canals. But quite enough to convince Brian that, with Sandra, he should spend the morning bird-watching from the catamaran – and ship-watching from the catamaran. There were quite enough of both passing by to keep him well occupied, and well away from the heterodont dentition of crocodiles (they have, as Brian had learnt, discernible molars, incisors and canine teeth).

Anyway, after another *al fresco* lunch, it was time for the *Discovery* to make its way to the north of Gatun Lake and to the three-step Gatun Locks. Yes, it was time to complete the transit of the Panama Canal and for the *Discovery* to make its way into the Caribbean, the prospect of which ensured that all its passengers were once again assembled on its outside decks. Clearly, none of them wanted to miss a second of this next encounter with the canal's remarkable engineering.

This time it was going to be different. Rather than following a freighter into the locks, as had happened yesterday, on this occasion the *Discovery* was going to be the first vessel in, and behind it would come an even larger vessel than had been encountered yesterday, a grain-carrier presumably on its way to somewhere in that threatened Western world. Initially, Brian was unaware of this, and his attention was held by the open lock chamber now directly ahead of the *Discovery*, and a big blue and white car-carrier in the chamber ahead of this. It looked just like the mid-section of an ocean liner that had lost all of its superstructure. It was really not very elegant at all.

Nor were the containers apparently gliding by in the nearby forest. They weren't doing this on their own, of course, but with the help of one of the super-sized container ships passing into the new super-sized lock chambers that had been built parallel to the original pair. With tall vegetation between the old and the new, it was only the containers piled on top of the ship that were visible and not the ship itself. And whilst certainly not an elegant sight it was a rather surreal sight and one which found itself being photographed by all those on board (although nobody, of course, used it as a backdrop for a selfie).

The photographers' attention was then caught by the car-carrier. The *Discovery* had now entered the lock and had come to a stop near its front end – very close to the back end of the *Pyxis Leader* in the chamber in front. This gave all aboard the *Discovery* a wonderful view of this block of maritime metal making its way into the next chamber – and the incredibly tight fit of this metal within the lock walls. Forget having difficulty in squeezing an MP's humility between the two; you couldn't have squeezed his conscience between the two – even if you'd been able to find it.

Well, this was all genuinely fascinating stuff, and better was to come – in the shape of the *Zen Noh Grain Pegasus,* the intriguingly named grain carrier that was to be the *Discovery's* companion though the Gatun set of locks. It had now appeared; a huge fat monster of a ship that would clearly only just fit into the lock, steaming forwards and as yet without the braking controls provided by the mules. There were not yet any cables in use, and there wouldn't be until two maniacs had rowed themselves out into the path of the monster (in a very small boat) in order to receive a couple of ropes thrown by its crew, which would then allow the connection of cables to the mules. It all looked very Heath Robinson and very bloody dangerous. But presumably the two paid maniacs had done this thing a thousand times before and, indeed, were able to make it seem very matter of fact and no more dangerous than a punt on the Cam. And they did have safety-helmets on, an almost infallible protection against the consequences of being run over by several tens of thousands of tonnes of metal.

This was a big ship. It needed two mules on either side at its bow, and two either side at its stern. Eight in all – obviously. And this was very good news as far as Brian was concerned. After all, that mass of ship was now sailing directly towards him, and he was standing on a small catamaran with unknown crumpling credentials. He had no desire to be squashed by a big grain-carrying tub, and the chances of this happening were significantly reduced by the presence of the extra braking power afforded to the tub by eight mules. And this wasn't an entirely ridiculous concern. The *Never Zeh Noh* was now getting closer and closer and filling more and more of the lock with its prodigious size. And had anybody really measured its length – accurately?

Of course somebody had, and with the help of those helpful mules, the grain carrier came to a dignified stop several yards away from the *Discovery's* stern. And soon it and the *Discovery* were on their way down.

It was all textbook stuff – through each of the Gatun Locks' three chambers – and all as thrilling as it had been the previous day. And why wouldn't it be? Giant gates, giant locks, giant lock walls, giant amounts of water, and giant ships. Indeed, as the *Discovery* was finally leaving the last lock chamber, the 'giant-ship' aspect of this oversized performance came to the fore. Not only was the *Discovery* situated just below the mighty *Zeh Noh*, but in the parallel chamber to the right, which had not yet been emptied of its water, was the equally massive *Altair Sky*, a huge red beast that loomed above the *Discovery* like a block of flats – or at least like a big red ship that hadn't yet been lowered to the *Discovery's* level. These two ships together, the *Always Zeh Noh* and the *Altair Sky*, put the seal on this incredible transit of the Panama Canal, an experience that would remain in Brian's memory for a very long time to come. As too would the *Discovery's* passage under the 'Atlantic Bridge'.

No. Brian had not been mistaken here. There are only two bridges over the Panama Canal: the Bridge of the Americas and the Centennial Bridge, both of which are to the south of Gatun Lake. And the Atlantic Bridge is not a bridge at all, because it is not yet complete. It soon will be, and its finished form is already easy to discern. It is something called a 'double pylon, cable stayed' bridge, and that means it has two huge concrete pylons, each supporting through an elegant screen of cables the two main spans that make up the central part of the construction. Or at least they will make up the central part of the construction when they're completed. As Brian saw straightaway, they are not yet there and the 'bridge' is currently two enormous pylons, each supporting a 'floating' span of roadway, both of which fail to meet either their elevated approach road or the other span. That is to say, there is presently an approach road, a gap, a span, a gap, a span, a gap, and an approach road. Indeed, it could be the finished product of a government ministry, but in fact it is the nearly completed work of some people who clearly knew what they were doing. Not only did this unfinished work already look pretty stylish, but it also looked as though the currently separate bits of the bridge would eventually meet up perfectly, and the bridge would probably work.

Anyway, it was certainly a fascinating sight, and in its work-in-progress state added greatly to the sense of bustle at this Caribbean end of the canal. Beneath it were passing any number of large ships on their way into or out of the canal, and sitting further out to sea were even more ships. Brian assumed that the members of this large flotilla were waiting their turn to transit the canal, but there again they might well have been redundant ships waiting instead for a call to be used. Brian's knowledge of the current health of the shipping industry didn't enable him to decide. What he had no problem in deciding, however, was that the *Discovery*, as it made its way into open water, would have been far happier to have stayed in the canal.

The Pacific Ocean had been… pacific. The waters of the canal and even of Gatun Lake had been delightfully unruffled. But this Caribbean chunk of the Atlantic Ocean was anything other than pacific or unruffled. It was full of lots of waves, and the double hull of the *Discovery* was not best designed to deal with these waves. (In fact, Brian suspected it was why it had been banished from its birthplace in Tasmania, and sent to a location where for most of the time it could make do with the maritime capabilities of a flat-bottomed barge.)

No matter. Because after the skipper had coaxed his catamaran through the bumpy waters of the Caribbean – due west – for only a little while, he was doing a left turn (south) to take his craft into the calm waters of the Chagres River. And these waters could not have been calmer. Because, as all those on board who had being paying attention to their transit across Panama would have recalled, the Chagres River had been dammed over a century before to create Gatun Lake and the necessary reservoir for the Panama Canal. This meant that the 'Chagres River' into which the *Discovery* had turned was a freshwater river no more, but instead a long, narrow (mostly saltwater) inlet from the sea. The only freshwater it received was that which was released through the Gatun Dam to provide electricity for the operation of the canal. The Chagres here no longer really flowed and it no longer provided a route into the interior of Panama, but just a much shorter route to the large earthen dam just a few miles upstream. In fact, it was neither fish nor fowl, neither a real river nor a natural inlet – but it was very attractive all the same.

It looked like one's standard large tropical river, edged with uninterrupted steamy tropical forest, and promising all those aboard the *Discovery* a genuine away-from-it-all experience. There was, after all, no river traffic on this non-river, and for the forthcoming night and apparently all of tomorrow morning the *Discovery's* passengers would be able to wallow in an undisturbed episode of tropical delight. And they'd probably all have a drink as well.

They did. Then they had dinner. And for Brian and Sandra that meant dinner with Angela and William and Linda and Wayne (they still hadn't learnt). Needless to say, Brian had soon revealed his soapbox from beneath his chair, and soon after this he was revealing the prescribed topic of conversation that would accompany this evening's meal. Quite simply it was 'what one would choose to put into one's own personal manifesto'. When asked to clarify this by Linda, he explained that what he had in mind was an exploration of what all those around the table might promise prospective voters if they were standing for public office. What legislative changes would they pursue as priorities if and when they were elected?

His companions seemed to understand what he meant, but before they could even get a word out, he sprang back in with a number of restrictions which he wished to impose – which took no account of the American and Canadian nationalities of the majority of his co-diners. He did not, he explained, want anybody to default to the obvious choices, which for him were six in number and were as follows.

Number one was the introduction of laws to recognise the desire by a majority of reasonable people for the availability of assisted dying. That was a no-brainer. Then there was the passing of legislation to renounce the regrettable membership of international agreements concerning a nation's responsibilities to refugees, which ignored that nation's responsibilities to its own citizens. (Associated legislation would deal with re-entry into such agreements when they had been brought up to date to recognise the three-fold increase in the world's population since their original introduction.) After this it was changing the law to bring in some equivalence between public sector pensions and those the private sector could afford, followed by radical changes to the law to provide public health through a personal insurance system that put back in place personal responsibility for one's health. One would no longer be able to burden others with the cost of one's bad habits. Number five was the introduction of tax legislation to penalise, rather than reward, excessive breeding. And finally, there was the legislation that was needed to prevent the charitable giving away of somebody else's money – which would stop ineffective and destructive foreign aid in its tracks.

At this point, Sandra was looking at the ceiling of the dining room and Wayne was looking disturbed. Had he really heard all that stuff? But before any perplexity was resolved, Brian was inviting contributions from his prospective politicians, and Angela lost no time in coming forward. She proposed that there might be a need for a law that demanded silence at the dinner table from any representative of an ex-colonial power. And then William pitched in by suggesting that there might be merit in a law that required certain ex-colonial powers to pay reparations to his own country to recognise the pain and anguish that had been imposed on it by the appearance of both Piers Morgan and James Corden on US TVs. Before Brian could assemble any challenge to these proposals, Linda came in with a new law that would require the UK to take Justin Bieber (permanently) in exchange for Canada retaining the Queen as its head of state. Brian tried to stem the flow at this point, but then Sandra came in with two of her own suggestions for new legislation. One was a new law that would require all husbands to learn how to operate a washing machine, and the other was to require not just all husbands, but all men, to sit on the loo to pee. Standing up to pee into a WC – and thereby not promoting the equality of the sexes – would become a serious offence, with guaranteed in-*khazi*-ration for repeat offenders.

Brian knew he was lost. It was bad enough to have all these ridiculous suggestions thrown his way, but to have Sandra making a dreadful toilet joke… well, that was the end. There was only one thing he could do: take up the job of putting together those manifesto promises himself.

And he'd start with something not too controversial: a change to the age at which one was eligible to vote…

'It has often been debated,' he started, 'as to whether eighteen years of age represents the appropriate time at which citizens of various democracies are given the right to vote – particularly when old-fashioned childhood seems to be so early discarded these days…'

'You're not going to suggest it should be reduced to sixteen?' interrupted an alarmed-sounding Sandra.

'Good God, no,' responded Brian. 'I'd bring in legislation to raise it to thirty-two, an age when the current generation might just be on the point of leaving its new-fashioned childhood…'

'Are you serious?' asked Wayne.

'Deadly. And let me ask you something, Wayne. Do you think you should have been given the vote at eighteen?'

'Well, I'm not sure…'

'I am,' responded Brian. 'I know I shouldn't have been given the vote at eighteen. God, I certainly shouldn't have been given it at twenty-one – when I was still at university – because I knew nothing of anything. And then for the whole of my twenties I insulated myself against anything remotely political by immersing myself in my career and by generally enjoying myself. And I was still a complete political ignoramus when I entered my thirties. And I simply cannot believe that young people know anything like enough about anything to make even half-reasonable voting decisions before they're "almost mature". You know, lots of early civilisations were run by a panel of elders. Some still are. And there's a reason for that. They know a hell of a lot more than their juniors do. They've seen it all before. They've got a good idea of what works and what doesn't work. And their heads are not full of dewy-eyed nonsense, unrealistic notions, childlike ideas, misinformed ideas – and pink, fluffy candyfloss. It's pretty dangerous to allow young people to have kids. But to allow them to have the vote is far, far worse. No. There's no question about it. My manifesto would include the promise to raise the voting age to thirty-two – or maybe thirty-five – and maybe they'd also have to take an exam. You know, to see whether they've even a clue about what they're voting for. I'd have to give that a little more thought…'

'How,' asked William, 'are you going to get elected – by people who you are promising to disenfranchise immediately?'

'Fraud. Which brings me to my next manifesto promise: the fraud that has been committed on the English people for centuries – in the shape of the so-called United Kingdom.'

Sandra let out a not necessarily theatrical but definitely very loud sigh.

'Yes, I would pursue legislation that would deliver a referendum to the English people, intended to discover whether they wanted to dissolve the UK. Or at least prune it back a bit. You know, to rid themselves of what are increasingly a load of spongers and ingrates…'

'You can't say that,' interjected Sandra.

'Possibly not on the other side of the Irish Sea, but I think I'm OK in Blighty…'

'Brian…'

'OK. I'll tone it down. Number three: make nuisance phone-calling a capital offence. If these bloody pests think so little of us that they think nothing about ruining our days, then I think we should think very little of them. Especially when they're gone…'

'Oh my God…'

'Number four: put into law the requirement to provide the necessary health care and counselling to all those who are suffering from a belief in socialism. And number five: put the VAT on those oversized false eyelashes up to 1000% – not just for the benefit of all those who are exposed to them but also for the benefit of the poor misguided souls who choose to wear them…'

'And I wonder who the guy was who invented VAT,' interrupted Sandra. 'And I wonder whether he – and it was bound to be a "he" – knew that he'd invented something that might last as long as we do, something that will still be around for as long as *Homo sapiens* are around. Or maybe even longer…'

That was it. The signal had been sent. It was the end of Brian's performance at the dinner table. He would now have to wait until he was back with Sandra in their cabin to embark on his next routine. And this he did just as soon as he and Sandra were tucked up in bed.

'As regards what has disappeared from our lives,' he began, 'the next episode has to be "free speech".'

'In England?' Sandra asked.

'Yes. In England, the very home of free speech. Where free speech was once the hallmark of our culture – but not anymore.'

Sandra did the decent thing. She foolishly asked him to expand on his statement.

'Well...' he began in a very Robert Peston sort of way, 'we're all told that free speech is something we're all entitled to, but in fact we're only entitled to it as long as we don't use it. If you actually open your mouth and say what you think, you'll soon get buried in a bloody avalanche. You'll be accused of being racist or ignorant or intolerant or bigoted or prejudiced or just hopelessly unreformed – or of being a misogynist, a chauvinist pig, an Islamophobe or a xenophobe. But not often a misanthrope because that word never trends on Twitter. But the fact remains that free speech no longer exists. One cannot say – in public – what one thinks. And if one does, one will quite often feel not just the wrath of the Twitter brigade but even the long arm of the law. Even if what one has said is patently true.

'Truth is no longer legitimate if it conflicts with the edicts of political correctness. It matters not at all that you might want to point out the nonsense or even the corrosive effect of the latest manifestation of sickeningly virtuous, super-sensitive, super-inclusive bollocks that these days passes for some sort of received wisdom. Because if you make so much as a peep that deviates from the rigid code of "what one is supposed to think" you're in really hot water. It's not so much a case of free speech but more a case of free rein – given to all those in the battalions of the thought police (and sometimes the real police) to do everything they can to make sure you don't step out of line again. Free speech is now just a private affair, something one can indulge in when one is in the company of like-minded friends. It is no longer a public undertaking – which means it is no longer really free speech at all. We have lost it. And those growing up in this unpleasantly supervised society will never even know we once had it. That there was once a time when one could say what one liked, and of course when one could offend all those who so deserved to be offended. Of which, I am sorry to say, there are now more than ever before…'

Sandra must have guessed that this was the end of this evening's lecture, so she chose to confirm this with an almost complimentary remark.

'I can only agree,' she said. 'But what can one do?'

Brian grinned.

'One can move onto my second topic. As I'm sure you'll remember, I did promise you a double helping this evening.'

Sandra let out a small groan, but it wasn't going to stop her husband. He was off again before she could draw breath.

'Right,' he started, 'non-self-centring-steering…'

'What!'

'You must remember – just about – that after the war, cars were still made with a steering system that didn't self-centre. You know, if you went round a corner, the wheel wouldn't then slip back through your hands. Instead you'd have to turn it back yourself. If you didn't do that you'd just continue to turn and probably mount the pavement.'

'God, Brian, that was very a long time ago…'

'Yep, but I still remember driving such a car: an old Austin A40. And I also remember how difficult it was compared to all the self-centring-steering cars we have now. It was a real trial, especially before the days of power-steering.'

'So your point is? If you have a point.'

'I do. You see, self-centring-steering – and power steering and anti-lock brakes and independent suspension – were all good things. And they were good things because they helped people to drive. But then the car makers ran out of useful innovations and they started to make their cars with a whole crop of innovations which were designed to help people *not* to drive – probably starting with that ridiculous cruise control, which only a moron would choose to engage. But since then it's got significantly worse. So now you can get cars that can stop themselves, cars that can park themselves – and soon they'll apparently come with satnav systems that remind you to turn the wheel when you're turning a corner and point out those really rare hazards on the road, otherwise known as other cars and bicycles. And it won't be too much longer before there'll be cars that massage yer triceps, put a crease in yer trousers, wipe yer bum and decide how you should spend yer day. Not only are all these more recent innovations robbing us of our ability to drive – presumably as a softening-up process for the arrival of genuinely driverless cars – but they're also robbing us of our ability to operate as independent sentient beings. As, I must say, is a load of other modern and completely insidious technology.

'We should have realised something when that cruise control stuff came in; that there's a conspiracy to make us all redundant...'

'So not only are we all being silenced,' interrupted Sandra, 'but we are also all being enfeebled as a species, reduced to no more than infantilised drones. And it all started with cruise control...'

'I rest my case,' responded a grinning Brian. 'But I don't regret the passing of non-self-centring-steering. That was just a fag. Or am I not allowed to say that these days?'

He grinned again, and then it was time for sleep. He and Sandra were both tired. After all, not only had it been a long day, but over the past two days both of them had crossed a whole bloody continent. It was little wonder they were tired...

19.

     ric wasn't really sure to start with. With his poor eyesight and his even poorer sense of hearing he thought he might be mistaken. But no, he wasn't. It was another one of those things he'd seen last week and the week before that. It was floating on the river and it contained the same sort of odd-looking animals, big things with bare faces, some of them with scraps of hair on their head – as far as he could tell – and all of them with fur on their bodies that didn't look quite like fur at all. It looked more like a covering of loose skin and it came in all sorts of colours. Yes, they were just really weird to look at and even weirder in their behaviour. They didn't do anything. They just seemed to stare, or some of them held something up to their face but they didn't seem to do anything with it. They just held it. No, it simply wasn't the sort of behaviour you'd expect from an ocelot, say – and this was bloody good news. They might be mildly irritating, and especially at this early hour in the morning when he was barely awake, but they didn't seem at all dangerous. Eric didn't feel the need to hurry away. Instead, he decided he'd just hang around where he was and simply wait for them to go – just like the others had before.

Although he also decided that he wouldn't start his breakfast until they'd gone…

'Look,' said Brian to his wife, 'it's just over there. On that lower branch. You can see his head if you lean towards me.'

'Got it!' exclaimed Sandra. 'Our first sloth of the day and it's barely 7.00.'

She was spot on. José had loaded his little boat with eight of the *Discovery's* passengers at 6.30 and had taken it slowly downriver in the hope of finding some early-morning wildlife. And not only had he found quite a few birds for them but he had now found this brown-throated sloth, one of the world's four species of three-toed sloths and one of the world's most adorable animals. In fact, Brian had previously given serious consideration to being reincarnated as a sloth – if that ever became an option – although he had yet to make a final decision. He found their appearance and their very low metabolism extremely attractive, but there were a few downsides. He didn't think he'd be too keen on their diet (especially all those leaves) and he wasn't completely bowled over by the thought of going to the loo only once a week. And you'd even have to climb down from your tree to do it – which, for a sloth, must be a very slow and a very tedious job. Oh, and then there are things like ocelots and harpy eagles that might want to eat you and countless bugs, ticks and mites that might want to eat off you. So not a straightforward decision at all, despite their wonderfully slow life and their wonderfully enchanting appearance.

Maybe instead he should be an arboreal anteater…

Yes, the other boat full of the catamaran's remaining guests had found something in the vegetation on the other side of the river, and José was pretty sure it was an anteater. They were known to be here, and whilst difficult to find they did tend to lurk around the river's edge, just like the brown-throated sloth. He, incidentally, was now moving – almost imperceptibly – and Brian suspected he had become aware of his audience finally leaving, and he simply wanted to get on with his day, and probably have a bite to eat. Brian was entirely correct.

Anyway, it was now anteater time. The other boat had moved on and José took his own boat to take up its position in order to provide his own charges with a view of this remarkable creature. And it was remarkable. It was a northern tamandua anteater, an animal of about forty-five inches in length with pale yellow fur over most of its body except for a distinctive patch of black fur over its back, flanks and shoulders, which looks very much like a black anteater vest. Oh, and it has a prehensile tail and a very long snout – all the better for sucking up all those termites and ants, 9,000 of which it apparently gets through every day.

This diet was one of the reasons that Brian had not seriously considered being reincarnated as an anteater. Not only was it the antithesis of a varied and interesting diet, but it would also inevitably contain a lot of formic acid. And he could never have coped with that. It would have made his breath smell something awful...

Brian and Sandra had never seen an arboreal anteater before, but only a giant anteater (in Venezuela). Rhona, of course, had seen both these varieties – and a southern tamandua anteater as well. She informed them of this as she shared breakfast with them back on the *Discovery*, and then went on to try to recall how many sloths she'd seen before and of which varieties these had been. And she even managed to introduce her encounters with ocelots and jaguars into her uncalled-for verbal communiqué, and Brian was soon regretting his return to the *Discovery*. He would have been better off staying out in that little boat with José, and eschewing breakfast entirely. He might even have seen an ocelot or a jaguar.

That, of course, would have been highly unlikely, and given that it had now decided to rain for a while, extremely unlikely if not impossible. He would instead have to comfort himself with the thought that breakfast would soon be over and that he could have a morning at leisure before a promised excursion after lunch. This was to be to some historic ruins at the mouth of the Chagres River. They had been glimpsed when the *Discovery* had entered the river yesterday, but now they were going to be explored – in the hottest part of the day!

The captain of the catamaran had brought his vessel downriver and it was now moored in sight of the 'target' ruins, the quite considerable amount of stonework that once was the formidable 'Fort San Lorenzo'. A fort had first been built here in the sixteenth century in order to provide protection to the Caribbean end of an early cross-isthmus trail, a trail that brought plundered gold from Peru to Spain's storehouses in its Atlantic-coast ports. Indeed, this trail in the rainy season was mostly the Chagres River. So choosing a site for a fortification on a promontory overlooking the river's mouth was a bit of a no-brainer. So too was the need for such a fortification. Gold attracts pirates, and around 1560 there was no shortage of all sorts of piratical types around the coast of Panama, and they weren't here looking for sloths and anteaters. They were here to rob Spain of the gold it had robbed from Peru.

However, it wasn't until 1670 that the fort succumbed. This it did at the hands of that well-known buccaneer, slaveholder, landowner and latterly Lieutenant Governor of Jamaica, one Sir Henry Morgan. He obliterated the place and then rubbed salt into Spain's wounds by using San Lorenzo as his base for invading Panama City. He was a bit of a menace really and he certainly could never have retired to the Costa del Sol to enjoy his ill-gotten gains.

Anyway, notwithstanding this reversal to and removal of their fortunes, the Spanish constructed a new fort on the site in 1680 – eighty feet above the sea – and this new, improved fortification allowed the town of Chagres to be established under its protection. This worked quite well, and when in 1740 another British gentleman by the name of Admiral Edward Vernon attacked the new San Lorenzo fort and its neighbouring fort up the coast at Portobelo, it was Portobelo's fort that was destroyed and San Lorenzo's that survived. Consequently, for a little while at least, Chagres became Spain's principal port on the Atlantic coast of the isthmus. It's even rumoured that it got its own MacDonald's and Central America's very first Walmart (although there is some academic debate concerning the veracity of these claims).

Unfortunately – for Chagres and for Fort San Lorenzo – the good times were not destined to last. Spain soon abandoned its trails across the isthmus, preferring instead to take its booty around Cape Horn, and the fort and the town both receded in importance. Even a much later revival in traffic following the advent of the California gold rush and the institution of a Chagres River steamboat service couldn't save them, and ultimately the Panama Railway and, of course, the Panama Canal killed them off entirely. All that now remain are the ruins of the town and the fort (contained within the 30,000-acre 'San Lorenzo Protected Area'), and possibly a few old piratical ghosts. And one can only hope, for the sake of those ghosts, that they don't much mind the heat.

Yes, all the *Discovery's* passengers had now been landed on a jetty that would allow them to embark on a half-mile walk through a forest to the ruins of Fort San Lorenzo – and it became apparent immediately that this hottest part of the day just after lunch was going to be exceptionally hot, although, according to José, not exceptionally hot for this little patch of Panama.

Brian was soon very damp. He was able to clock a few monkeys and a few birds on his way to the fort, but only by frequently wiping his spectacles and even more frequently blotting his brow. He did not, however, manage to see his first ever armadillo, an animal that had been inconsiderate enough to cross the trail through the forest while he had been looking the other way. He was not at all pleased. Neither was he ecstatic at the prospect of exploring the ruins of the fort under a blazing sun and in oven-like temperatures. It really was hotter than ever, and the fort really was in ruins and offered virtually no shade whatsoever.

Well, he and Sandra did manage a bit of a perambulation and the fort did hold a certain degree of interest. In particular, one could gaze at the intricate stonework that remained – and the scale of this stonework, which was huge – and wonder how on Earth anybody had been able to work for much more than a few minutes in this punishing heat to put all the original stonework together. Brian wouldn't have managed even a few minutes, and if he had tried he would soon have ended up as a desiccated husk. By just standing in this heat, he was flowing more than that nearby Chagres River. It was all worth it though. On the way back to the jetty he caught a fleeting glimpse of a real armadillo!

Back on the catamaran, it was time for an immediate long and tepid shower – and time for the catamaran's master to take it out to sea again in order to return it to the mouth of the Panama Canal near the city of Colón. This is where it would moor overnight, before it made its way further east along the coast in the morning. Fortunately, Brian had finished his shower before the *Discovery* made open water. When it did, it reminded all on board that it was not designed for open water. Indeed, Brian was very happy when it had completed its short journey and was parked in the shelter of a breakwater near that uncompleted Atlantic Bridge. Although, there again, he was just a little bit concerned to be parked quite so close to the busy shipping lanes at the approach to the Panama Canal. Hell, the *Discovery* was tiny, and most of the ships using the canal were anything but tiny. Indeed, moored just a few hundred yards away was an immense ocean liner. And what if it strayed from its moorings overnight or, more likely, one of those scores of ships passing by didn't quite succeed in passing by but instead made an unannounced arrival – on top of the *Discovery*?

Well, there was only one thing to do – or maybe two things to do. The first was to have an early drink, and the second was to ensure that this last dinner aboard the catamaran was shared with Angela and William and Linda and Wayne and, of course, number one wife – who on this occasion was the first to suggest a topic to kick off the over-dinner conversation. And what she suggested was that all those around the table should present their view of what might constitute their very own personal version of heaven. If they could manage to suspend their likely disbelief in any sort of afterlife for just a while, what, she wanted to know, would be their preferred version of nirvana? She was careful to point out that 'an infinite life with my partner' would not be allowed, on the basis that co-terminus departures could not be guaranteed, and even if they could, who was to say that one partner might not end up in a very different destination? She was also careful to point out that their choices would not be broadcast beyond the dinner table. After all, revealing one's personal paradise preferences would be a very personal thing, and even if they were ever reported in a book, they would have to be anonymised. Which is why the six heavenly choices below are not attributed to their individual owners but instead are presented in a way that only betrays each owner's gender – and not even how serious each owner was about his or her choice…

One of the males at the table was the first to reveal all. And his idea of heaven was basically an infinite indulgence in hedonism. Not for him choirs of angels and fluffy clouds, but more the never-ending pursuit of pleasure – for which an infinite afterlife was more than ideal. After all, he pointed out, the great Jeremy Bentham believed the value of pleasure to be its intensity multiplied by its duration. So what better way of spending an infinite duration than by really going for it on the pleasure front and thereby getting the very best value possible out of one's time after death. Good food, good wine, good sensual experiences of every kind imaginable, and probably good cigars and cigarettes that could no longer do one any harm – and the ability to let one's desires flourish in the broadest possible terms. Oh, and all without one becoming satiated, overweight, jaded or bored. Obviously. This, he maintained, was an honest choice, and a choice many had already made for their time here on Earth – even if they couldn't quite manage it, and there were always associated detrimental consequences, like getting fat or arrested…

Well, this proposal received a rather lukewarm response from the other five at the table, and spurred one of them to make a rather more laudable proposal. This was to spend one's afterlife taking on a series of never-ending challenges and being able, through a combination of hard work, ingenuity and imagination, to overcome these challenges and thereby earn oneself a repeated sense of satisfaction – *ad infinitum*. She (and it was a she) said that she could never abide the thought of some sort of passive heaven, the sort where one sat around either adoring someone or even stuffing one's face with heavenly ambrosia all the time. For her it had to be all about satisfying oneself through doing something, and what better to do than to overcome challenges all the time, challenges that were difficult enough and varied enough never to pall and never to become even marginally tedious. So it certainly wouldn't be like doing an infinite series of Sudoku puzzles...

The next contributor was keen to reveal a personal heaven that combined elements of those already revealed, but in a very specific way. For her (yes, it was another of the women at the table), paradise would consist of a series of 1,000-piece jigsaws – of natural scenes taken from around the globe – and the reward for completing them would be an extended visit to observe these natural scenes and their natural fauna and flora at first hand (as a sort of ghostly naturalist who didn't need to bother with a rucksack). Having completed this visit, she would then return to comfortable surroundings and listen to some of her favourite music before falling asleep. Waking again, another jigsaw would await her, and the same cycle of jigsaw, 'safari', music and sleep would kick off again. Oh, and of course this experience would never become stale and she would never not want to get out of bed to tackle that next awaiting jigsaw.

This version of heaven met with an unusual degree of approval, as did the next, which was another one that relied on the beauty of the natural world and its rich and varied wildlife. It was very simple. It was spending a day in one of the extremely agreeable camps in the Okavango Delta – over and over again until the end of time. Each day would entail an early rise to take in the African sunrise, a game drive to observe whatever birds and animals revealed themselves before breakfast, a late breakfast (with a glass of lager), a spot of bird-watching from the camp, a simple lunch, a siesta, another rewarding game drive, and then a delicious dinner with good wine and good companions before retiring to bed, weary but deeply satisfied. The same routine the next day would uncover new natural wonders and deliver the same sense of intense pleasure – as would the next day and the next *ad infinitum*. And there wouldn't be any biting insects and the G&Ts would never run out.

This proposal was from a man at the table. The next was from the final woman. This consisted of an infinite series of wishes. She explained that she couldn't possibly decide what would be her perfect heaven, now, so needed a heaven that would allow her to do what she wanted, as she wanted to do it. And that, therefore, her perfect nirvana would be one where she could wish as she chose as she went along. Maybe, she said, she might want to talk to Churchill one day, but the next day she might want to bathe in ass's milk and after that take a trip to the moon. If every one of her wishes came true, she would be able to do this, and she would even be able to conjure up Paul Newman – just for dinner, you understand – and then maybe solve the 'theory of everything' by finally devising a coherent theoretical framework of physics that fully explains and properly reconciles all physical aspects of the universe. Although she would have no facility to pass this back to those still struggling with the enigma back on Earth…

'Not bad' was the general consensus on this version of heaven, and it received particular praise from the last contributor, who now went on to reveal his perfect paradise. It would, he explained, be a sort of Promised Land for snoopers – but in a nice way. Because what he envisaged was the ability to visit any place on Earth at any time in the past, present or future as the archetypal 'fly on the wall'. He wanted to see, for example, how a Neanderthal family provided itself with amusement – if it did provide itself with amusement. He wanted to know what it was like to land on a D-Day beach, what it was like to be on a Space Shuttle – and what Trump and Putin actually said to each other in Helsinki. And then he'd really like to know how Europe got on when Europeans had become a minority on that continent and how mankind ended up in the twenty-fifth century – if there was still any of mankind left alive then.

Well, this was a valid and interesting proposal, but the general opinion was that the jigsaw and Botswana versions of heaven would take some beating. Although, there again, there was very little to choose between all six of the ideas that had been put forward.

However, would it be the same for the six diners' very own ideas of Hell? Yes, inevitably, Brian had used his wife's uplifting idea to launch his own assault on his table companions, which simply asked them to reveal what it was that would constitute their very own worst visions of Hell. And with the same provisos. That is to say, their revelations would not be broadcast beyond the dinner table – and Hell could not consist of an infinite existence shared with one's spouse…

After a little hesitation, Brian's suggestion was accepted – even if a little reluctantly by a minority of the table – and the first personal Hell was revealed. It was a woman doing the revealing and what she disclosed to the other diners was that an infinite period of torture for her would be to live in an afterlife where everything was entirely superficial. Entertainment would be on tap, but it would be a never-ending series of ironically named reality shows, tinsel-draped dancing competitions and celebrity-stuffed panel games, none of which would contain even an iota of anything remotely genuine – just as they don't up here on Earth. The performers on these shows – and everybody else in this Hell – would be equally superficial. Not only in their boob-and-bum-augmented bodies, their distemper-embellished teeth and their surgically-enhanced pecs, but also in their manner, their faux overfriendliness and their exaggerated reaction to even the slightest stimulus to their small superficial brains. No one would have any real friends – but lots of so-called friends on social media. And social media would form the fundamental core of this Hell, and would be nothing more than a humungous compilation of superficial messages, superficial responses, superficial greetings, superficial 'likes' and superficial tripe. Nothing would have any worth and nothing would be of any significance or of any real interest. Stretching over infinite time, suggested the proposer, this could only be the very worst version of Hell.

Well, yes. But hadn't the proposer noticed, William observed, that she was already surrounded by such a Hell up here on Earth, and her very own Hell was just a lot more of the same. She had noticed, she said. But whilst she could presently avoid all this superficiality by the way she conducted her life, Hell would be her not being able to avoid it and having nothing else to turn to. William accepted this, and then it was time for the first male version of Hell.

This was being immersed not in superficiality but in ignorance, the sort of ignorance that Brian had himself discussed no more than a few days before and that was now the hallmark of so many of his fellow men (and women). This Hell would be sharing one's infinite afterlife with an infinite multitude of these ignoramuses, and having their ignorance on display without any respite whatsoever and without any hope that any of them would ever learn anything. None of them would ever crack percentages. None of them would ever know where their country of birth fitted onto a map of the world. None of them would ever know the difference between 'imply' and 'infer'. None of them would ever know how wilfully ignorant they were, having spent all their time on Earth studiously avoiding any sort of study and thereby successfully failing to learn anything worthwhile at all – and certainly not what the capital of Peru was…

One of the women at the table was clearly impressed by this idea that ignorance could constitute a Hell, but was eager to go just one step further – even if it meant a backhanded sort of acceptance of the idea of an afterlife, whether it be spent in heaven or in Hell. Because her idea of Hell was, she maintained, being trapped in the ultimate manifestation of ignorance – which was hard-core religion. She would dread, she explained, the thought of living in some sort of never-ending caliphate or some sort of fundamentalist, revivalist, more-than-a-little-out-of-their-brain-ist community that went on for ever – or an evangelical heaven that just didn't know when to stop evangelising. She then went on to say that it was bad enough that most of mankind on Earth today was locked into irrational (and ignorant) beliefs. But the idea that an infinity would have to be spent with only these sorts of people and with nobody who was rational, enlightened and 'normal' would, for her, be a really, really dismal sort of Hell.

So too, offered the next (male) contributor, would be a Hell run by Trump and largely managed on his behalf by a whole raft of ignorant, incompetent, so-called 'leaders', a whole bunch of morons who are currently engaged in screwing up the lives of most people here on Earth. Just imagine, he said, having to live for eternity under the direction of dickheads like Maduro or Duterte or any one of the dozens of tin-pot dimwits and blockheads who are currently in positions of power around the world. These dictators and 'democratically elected' despots have already shown how they can make life a Hell on Earth for billions of people in their relatively short lifetimes. So just imagine, he said, what they could do if they were given infinity to play with – and only Trump to regulate their behaviour and offer them advice. It would be a Hell in Hell, he added, and you might even be required to take Trump seriously, which of course would be just absolutely hellish but also completely impossible...

Well, these various versions of Hell were all valid in their own ways, admitted the next (female) contributor, but as far as she was concerned the ultimate Hell had to be a traditional Hell. Ignorance and superficiality – and religious zealots, along with Trump and any number of tyrants – were all very undesirable, but they were probably just about manageable. Whereas, she said, it was pretty difficult to imagine that anyone could cope with being roasted on a spit while being prodded with red-hot pokers for much more than about ten seconds, let alone an infinity. And if one placed a real Devil in this Hell and he was as diabolical as his PR suggested, then it seems that after ten seconds you wouldn't just faint, but instead you'd stay very much awake and very much in pain – for billions of years and then for billions of years more. And that, she argued, would be a Hell that could in no way be any worse. Although the final contributor begged to differ.

He thought you might get used to it. All that pain would resolve itself into something almost akin to pleasure – like when you find yourself humming along to the latest Kylie Minogue number. But what would be truly hellish, he proposed, would to be in a Hell that had only people and no other animals; a sort of eternal Elon Musk Mars colony, where it was considered tenable to have people living together without that crucial life-support system otherwise known as all the other creatures with whom we share this planet. It would be dreadful, he maintained; a denuded and deprived existence where our inability to exist with just our own kind would be plainly revealed, and one that would have to be endured until the end of time. It would be bad enough, he said, to have lost all the wonderful flora of the Earth. But also to have lost its entire fauna – other than, of course, other members of rapacious *Homo sapiens* – would be… well, horribly hellish, and for him the worst Hell of all.

William made another observation. He said that the final contributor had just presented a fairly accurate picture of the commonly held view of heaven – give or take the odd few virgins. So maybe he should be advised to live a terrible life in the hope of avoiding that heaven and instead ending up in someone else's version of Hell. Say the 'Ignorant' one or the 'Superficiality' number. Or maybe even Trump-world. He could at least have a laugh at the tosser…

It was a good observation by William, but it did have the disadvantage of letting loose an extended discussion on the leader of the Me-world, and this was not the right way to round off the last dinner together on the *Discovery*. So Brian eventually managed to bring the conversation around to sex and debauchery, which proved a far better and far more interesting conclusion. Then he stood up and gave a garbled vote of thanks to the catamaran's crew, and then he retired for the night. He hadn't forgotten that he still had another instalment of his 'what has disappeared from our lives' series to deliver to Sandra. And this final instalment was on the subject of 'marbles'.

'Do you remember "keepsies" and "marleys"?' he began.

'Eh?'

'Well, they're about the only terms I can remember from playing marbles. And I think "keepsies" was where you kept all the marbles you had won, and "marleys" was just the normal name we gave to playing marbles. But I can't remember very much else.'

'Ah, it's another episode of "what we have lost from our lives"!' exclaimed Sandra. 'How could I have been so slow?'

'Well, they are lost – sort of. I mean, I'm sure there are still some marble aficionados knocking around the place. You know, some middle-aged men with poor dress sense – but I doubt it's a popular diversion for the iPad generation. Apart from anything else, it's bound to have fallen foul of the Health and Safety brigade. You know, marbles probably now constitute a "swallow risk". Anyway, young kids are unlikely ever to have heard of the term "marleys" and they probably have no idea of how many idyllic hours could be spent flicking marbles around to get them into a hole.'

'Is that what you did?' asked Sandra. 'Was that the purpose of the game?'

Brian looked concerned. Then he spoke.

'You know, I'm not sure. All I remember is having a big collection of glass marbles in a green-and-white-striped drawstring bag, and that my favourite marbles were the small blue-centred ones. Although I did have a few other colours and a few marbles that were much larger than normal. Although I don't think we ever played with these. Competitive marleys – whatever it involved – was conducted with just the small ones…'

'So your point is?'

'Well, it's a great shame that it's not still a popular children's game. It was so engrossing and so enjoyable, and it got us out of the house and it probably even aided the development of our coordination skills…'

'Exactly like an iPad then?'

'Yeah. Exactly. In a world where absolutely everybody has lost their fucking marbles…'

That was it. Brian's final lesson had been delivered, and his wife would now be allowed to sleep – and to dream of a little spell of Earth-bound paradise in the morning, which, all being well, would very definitely be the antithesis of anybody's Hell.

20.

nfortunately, paradise was two hours of open sea away, which meant an interesting start to the day.

The *Discovery* had left the shelter of its mooring at first light, and had then sailed eastwards over a choppy sea on its way to Portobelo (where Admiral Edward Vernon had smashed up a fort). This meant that packing, abluting and breakfasting had to be conducted in a pitching and rolling vessel and at the expense of an extravagant use of calories. Bracing oneself against the motion of the catamaran – even when seated and cutting up one's omelette – proved to be a very energy-consuming pastime. Nevertheless, Brian and Sandra were both washed and fed and their cases were packed by the time the *Discovery* pulled into the calm waters of Portobelo Bay near Portobelo itself, and they were as prepared as they ever would be to deal with a round of goodbyes…

Yes, fifteen of the *Discovery's* passengers were scheduled to take a tour of the ruins of Portobelo's Fort (in the midday sun!) before then being taken back to Panama City by the Panama Canal Railway. However, the remaining two – Brian and Sandra – were to be taken to the other side of the bay in a small boat to spend two nights at a paradise resort by the name of 'El Otro Lado' – which means nothing more than 'The Other Side'. So quite fitting and quite clever really…

Anyway, this division of the party called for a copious round of heartfelt goodbyes together with the exchange of email and physical addresses – in addition to a round of goodbyes and thanks to the *Discovery's* hardworking crew. And then Brian and Sandra embarked on their three-minute journey across the bay, and were soon taking in their very first impressions of El Otro Lado. And there was quite a lot to take in.

As they had expected, it was a resort situated on the very edge of the bay and it was very small (it had only five cabins – or 'houses'). However, what neither of them had expected was that it was also one of the most colourful 'retreats' they had ever encountered. Within a little patch of tropical parkland, its owners had built a small collection of pastel-coloured cabins, each with a white roof and a multi-coloured deck – together with a white octagon-shaped main building set beyond a beautiful blue pool, surrounded by red, green and blue chairs. It was a (very colourful) joy to behold, and a taster for what was within these buildings.

Brian and Sandra had the 'Sea House', and the Sea House contained furniture, furnishings, paintings and countless artefacts that guaranteed that there wasn't one colour of the rainbow – or one colour not of the rainbow – that was missing. It was a 'balanced' riot of colour, and it worked, albeit it did have to play second fiddle to the agglomeration of colours – as represented by all the many outrageous artefacts – in the main building. This restaurant-cum-lounge and bar was more like a gallery of exuberant and flamboyant art than somewhere to eat and drink, and it, just like the Sea House, worked very well indeed. So too did the wood carvings all around the place, the generous use of mirror fragments in and around the buildings, the careful use of plants, and an extensive collection of decorative orchids.

This place was superb. Oh, and its only residents were Brian and Sandra. They had arrived in this Caribbean paradise, and they had it all to themselves. And, as would become apparent when they ate their first meal in the restaurant, the chow here was superb as well. What more could they possibly want?

Well, in the first place, the termination of the dreadful music which polluted the whole of the resort. It was mostly of the throbbing variety and its throbs could easily penetrate the walls of the Sea House. Brian had to ask one of the resort's staff to turn it off – on the reasonable grounds that he and Sandra were the resort's only guests, and one of them could well end up killing the other one if they didn't accede to his request. That refinement of paradise was a success, but nothing could be done about the other wrinkle in paradise, which was the presence of a ubiquitous profusion of sand-flies, sand-flies whose sole purpose in life was to bite.

Brian took only a little time to expose himself – or at least most of himself – when he went for a swim after lunch. All was well, while he was in the water, but as soon as he emerged and laid himself out on a sun-lounger to dry himself off, the biting got underway. And it was incessant and unbearable. Within only a few minutes he was back in the Sea House and considering how he was going to manage two more days of insect assault.

It wasn't easy. Swimming would have to be merely swimming, followed by a rapid retreat to the safety of the cabin's interior. Sitting out would be restricted to a fully-clothed exercise on the restaurant's veranda – trusting to the deterrent powers of G&Ts – and most of the rest of the time would be spent in the restaurant eating or in the Sea House reading or amusing oneself in other ways. In short, this end-of-holiday paradise looked good, but the only way it came up to scratch was literally, and as a result of the irritation caused by the numerous bites of sand-flies. It was, thought Brian, an object lesson to all those seeking to define what might be their version of heaven – or possibly even Hell. In fact, he went on to think, an eternity of insect bites might just qualify as one of the worst sorts of Hell imaginable.

Anyway, all good things – and not so good things – eventually come to an end, and just two days after arriving at El Otro Lado it was time to leave it. This entailed a boat ride to the other side of the bay and there being deposited in what proved to be the very sleepy town of Portobelo. Awaiting Brian and Sandra here was a minibus, its driver and his girlfriend, and the prospect of an interesting ride back to Panama City and then on to Tocumen International Airport and a flight back to Europe.

Well, the ride did prove interesting, but for all the wrong reasons. To start with, the tiny road that led out of Portobelo and along the Caribbean coast to Colón should have been charming if not idyllic. Instead it was not only charmless but it was also disgusting. Under a clear blue sky and set against the clear blue of the Caribbean Sea, the meandering road was edged on both sides with an unbroken line of filth. It wasn't just the odd discarded plastic bottle, but instead two 'pavements' of discarded plastic and other assorted garbage. It was even worse than the Pan-American Highway. If this wasn't dispiriting enough, there was then the city of Colón to send you into a spiral of dismay: urban ugliness drowning under a sea of garbage, with not so much as a smidgeon of elegance or grace to relieve it. No wonder, thought Brian, that it rarely if ever features on the tourist trail.

Nor, probably, does the workman-like dual carriageway back to Panama City (even if, like the driver of the minibus, one uses the wrong lane) and nor do the seedier tenements of Panama City one encounters at the end of this route. Yes, Brian and Sandra were nearly at their destination. And then, having negotiated – at speed – downtown PC, it was just a matter of speeding past the glitzy but soulless towers of 'Esplanade PC' and there they were, at Tocumen International Airport. Here, having checked in, they had a couple of hours to kill before their flight, and that meant a couple of hours for Brian to assemble his considered thoughts on the country in which he'd just spent the last three weeks of his life. And as is customary, he focused first on what had impressed him about this small Central American country.

Well, to start with, it had to be the survival of a fair amount of wilderness in Panama. Despite the best efforts of careless and consumptive mankind there were still patches of this country that managed to retain a covering of natural vegetation and, within this vegetation, host a multitude of natural gems. Even close to Panama City there was the wonderful Soberania National Park. And then there were the largely untouched areas in the immediate vicinity of both Tranquilo Bay Eco Lodge and Mount Totumas Lodge, to say nothing of the vast area that was the Darién region of the country. And in these near-pristine places one could find genuine wonders such as violet sabrewings, tody motmots and the incomparable rufous-crested coquette. Then there were the howler monkeys and the sloths and even arboreal anteaters. Panama still had extensive *real* riches, and even better they were still little visited. Neighbouring Costa Rica might be blessed with even more wild places, but it long ago learnt how to exploit them (sensitively) and this has led to a huge flood of overseas visitors. Panama lags behind, and so far there is just a trickle of visitors to this country, or at least to its natural realms. For this reason, Panama can offer a little sense of pioneering adventure as well as an extensive menu of both flora and fauna. Brian had been suitably impressed.

He had also been impressed with the Panama Canal. Indeed, nobody could fail to be impressed with this engineering marvel. It was just so stupendous an undertaking and so stupendous in its size. It dwarfed even the super-freighters that used it to ply their trade, and it had made most of the passengers of the *Discovery* feel as though they were aboard nothing more than a child's toy. Oh, and it all worked. The reservoir system in the shape of Gatun Lake successfully fed the whole canal system with all the water it needed throughout the year. The canal system itself was so well organised that all those huge ships that wanted to use it could be dealt with smoothly and as far as Brian could tell very efficiently. And the physical aspects of the canal, and in particular its massive locks, seemed to work perfectly. Their design and presumably their maintenance has guaranteed that the impossible amounts of water that need to be shifted each time a vessel passes through – are shifted without a hitch and without any sense of panic or drama. A watchmaker passing through this canal would probably really appreciate its faultless operation. And he might also be amused that it has helped in furnishing the world with one of the longest palindromes of all time…

Anyway, moving on… it would not be right, thought Brian, to ignore the fact that one of the most impressive aspects of Panama was that little toy catamaran that had been banished from Tasmania. The *Discovery* had been a joy, in every respect and not least in the quality of the food it provided to its passengers. This had been outstanding – and even better than the victuals on offer at Mount Totumas Lodge, which had themselves been excellent. Panama would do very well if it attempted to model itself on the *Discovery* in all sorts of ways – which might not be a very practical suggestion, but did lead Brian into those aspects of Panama that had not impressed him at all.

There are, of course, no prizes for guessing what not only failed to impress him about Panama, but what also appalled him about this place, and this was its concerted effort to look like a huge overflowing rubbish dump. Its urban areas – by and large – had clearly outlawed any adoption of municipal pride, and the residents of both the urban and more rural areas had taken this ban to heart at the domestic level as well. Scruffy, littered and irredeemably untidy had now become the national norm to be displayed on every home front and, even more so, on every highway and byway. The amount of filth on the edges of the Pan-American Highway was barely credible. The amount of filth on the edges of that road between Portobelo and Colón was actually genuinely *in*credible. It looked as though a real effort had been made to discard as much non-biodegradable trash along its route as was possible. So much, in fact, that if and when some geologists or archaeologists excavate this coastal strip a long way into the future, they may wrongly conclude that they have found either the world's first natural seam of plastic or a novel ceremonial route decorated with a tribe's precious collection of plastic heirlooms.

Of course, as already alluded to, Brian did have a bit of a thing about humanity's desire to leave a legacy of garbage around the world – and he had seen some truly awful examples of the result of this inclination on his previous travels (in such enlightened places as India, Morocco, The Gambia and [pre-apocalyptic] Syria). However, Panama would give any country on the planet a run for its money when it came to displaying such an egregious disregard for the environment. It could truly be called a first-rate despoiler and a true disciple of the creed of 'we just couldn't care'. One day, thought Brian, it might well totally disappear under the weight of its trash.

He also thought he might be putting the boot into this country a little too hard in respect of its slovenly habits. After all, it was not a super-rich nation, and any country does need some wealth to deal properly with its waste. But this thought led him on to another thought and this was the second aspect of Panama that had failed to impress him. It was the concentration of wealth in the hands of the few and the consequent impoverishment of the many. Noriega might not be around anymore, but Brian had heard rumours that no more than twenty families effectively owned the country. As they all seemed to live in Panama City, and feed off that city's questionable income streams, the rest of the country tended to get neglected – or exploited if this could add to the families' already established fortunes. One could certainly observe this concentration of wealth in the country's capital (even more plainly than one could see it in London), and one could equally see the absence of wealth in the rest of the nation. Indeed, the further one was from Panama City, the more obvious it was – as exemplified by the squalor of Bocas Del Toro in the extreme west and the neglect of the Darién region to the east. Residents of Cornwall and the Shetlands, thought Brian, would easily identify with this state of affairs, even if their circumstances were in no way as acute. Furthermore, these circumstances may not remain in place indefinitely – which fact led into Brian's next censure of this country.

It was the mirror image of the plus point concerning its wild places, and it was the unavoidable deduction that these remaining wild places were all under threat, either through not being cared for or, worse, by being eliminated entirely. In the first instance, 'preservation' was not high on the agenda of any of those back in Panama City who wielded power. Brian had not forgotten, for example, the paltry number of rangers who had to look after the wellbeing of huge tracts of the La Amistad International Park (located in the remote-from-Panama-City west of the country). Without proper protection none of these wilderness areas of the country were safe. However, there was an even greater threat, and this was the identification of a currently unspoilt area to be spoilt in the name of mammon. It was very apparent already in the Bocas Del Toro region, a wild area of Panama that borders the Caribbean and that will soon be seen as the next Caribbean Costa Blanca and soon after that developed out of existence. Where there are now acres of mangroves and a great deal of pleasing greenness, there will soon be hotels, condos, beach resorts and probably a good deal of trash. If one is ensconced in Panama City with a big stack of power and influence, one will probably not be too concerned with what has to be sacrificed in order to keep you in the style to which you have become accustomed – and another piece of this innocent world will be fed into the jaws of devastation.

OK, this was all getting a bit heavy. Even Brian was becoming aware of this. So he decided to turn away from the destruction of the natural world and to consider one other aspect of Panama that had failed to impress him. This was the shape and dress sense of too many of its population. In his mind, super-obesity was never a good idea, whether for a man or for a woman. But for super-super-obese women – of the sort encountered in that dreadful Panama City hotel (and elsewhere) – it was something else and something far worse. Fabric stretched to breaking point across the assembled bulges of gross womanhood was about as bad as it could get for Brian, but in this country it was definitely a wealth statement, and presumably a bit of a turn-on for the boys. How it could be either was a mystery to Brian, and another feature of this country that should be filed under 'less than impressive'.

Well, Brian and Sandra's flight had finally been called, which allowed Brian to clock up just two further thoughts before he and Sandra went off in search of their plane. The first was that despite all these negative aspects of Panama, there were also those earlier positives, and none of the negatives had stopped him enjoying his visit to this country in any way. It had been a wonderful and memorable experience. The second thought was that what had made it especially wonderful and memorable were the people he had met on this trip, people like Tatiana at Canopy Tower, people like Miguel and Oxana at the coffee *finca*, and people like José on the *MV Discovery*. Oh, and people who were visiting this country at the same time as he was. These people, above all others, had made his expedition to Panama an absolute delight.

Special mention would have to be made of the failed teetotallers at Canopy Lodge, Kathy and Mary, who had not only been splendid companions but who had also relieved his guilt concerning his intake of red wine. Then there had been Jim and Carolyn at Mount

Totumas, two people who exuded a wonderful blend of enthusiasm and charm, and who were approximately one trillion times more attuned to the delights of the natural world than their president back home will ever be. And finally, the four musketeers from the *Discovery:* Angela, William, Linda and Wayne, an assembly of the interesting and the good, shaped into four very different but very attractive North Americans. The catamaran had been superb. Their company aboard it had been superlative. And they'd all tolerated Brian's behaviour!

So, concluded Brian, there were lots of places on the planet that were better than Panama and lots that were infinitely worse. But no matter where one went, what really counted was with whom one shared the experience – whether intimately with a woman called Sandra or very amiably with, in this instance, a succession of really nice people from the USA and Canada.

And if any of this happy group of people didn't know about 'a man a plan a canal Panama' before they came to this country, they certainly knew it – courtesy of the verbose one – when they left.

And Sandra could only agree…

By the same author:

www.davidfletcherbooks.co.uk